WARRIOR • 142

BLUE DIVISION SOLDIER 1941–45

Spanish Volunteer on the Eastern Front

C. CABALLERO JURADO   ILLUSTRATED BY RAMIRO BUJEIRO

Series editors Marcus Cowper and Nikolai Bogdanovic

First published in Great Britain in 2009 by Osprey Publishing,
PO Box 883, Oxford, OX1 9PL, UK
PO Box 3985, New York, NY 10185-3985, USA
Email: info@ospreypublishing.com

Osprey Publishing is part of the Osprey Group.

Transferred to digital print on demand 2013

First published 2009
2nd impression 2010

Printed and bound by Cadmus Communications, USA.

A CIP catalogue record for this book is available from the British Library

ISBN: 978 1 84603 412 1

Editorial by Ilios Publishing Ltd, Oxford, UK (www.iliospublishing.com)
Page layout by PDQ Media
Index by Michael Forder
Typeset in Sabon and Myriad Pro
Originated by PDQ Media

Dedication
This book is dedicated to my wife, Laura, and my sons, Diego and Carlos.

Acknowledgements
The author gratefully acknowledges the invaluable assistance of César Ibáñez,
Martin Houghton, Pablo Sagarra, Manuel Liñán, Lucas Molina, Gonzalo Rodríguez,
Isabel Gonzálvez, the 'Fundación División Azul' and the 'Fundación Don Rodrigo'.

Artist's note
Readers may care to note that the original paintings from which the colour plates in this
book were prepared are available for private sale. All reproduction copyright whatsoever
is retained by the Publishers. All enquiries should be addressed to:

Ramiro Bujeiro, C.C. 281602, Florida, Argentina

The Publishers regret that they can enter into no correspondence upon this matter.

The Woodland Trust
Osprey Publishing is supporting the Woodland Trust, the UK's leading woodland
conservation charity, by funding the dedication of trees.

www.ospreypublishing.com

CONTENTS

BLUE DIVISION SOLDIER 1941–45

INTRODUCTION

Spain did not take part in either World War I or World War II. However, despite remaining neutral in the latter, many Spanish volunteers fought on the German side. The reason so many Spaniards decided to participate in this way has its roots in the Spanish Civil War of 1936–39. During that conflict, due to their anti-communist ideology, the 'Nacionales' (Nationalists) received aid from both Fascist Italy and Hitler's Third Reich. On the other side, the Popular Front was supported by the Soviet Union.

Without Soviet help, the revolutionary regime of the Spanish Popular Front (established in February 1936) would have collapsed a few months after the start of the Civil War. However, the USSR sent large quantities of modern armaments as well as military personnel to aid the Spanish Republican Army. The Soviet Union also organised the arrival of the International Brigades. During the Civil War, the left wing of the Partido Socialista Obrero Español (Spanish Socialist Workers Party), sympathetic to the Soviet Union, and the Spanish Communist Party, took almost complete control of the areas of Spain controlled by the Popular Front. These elements within the Popular Front were responsible for instigating a form of Stalinist terror, assassinating several thousand of their right-wing enemies.

When the Civil War ended in April 1939, those who had fought on the Nationalist side retained a deep hatred towards the Soviet Union and felt a sense of gratitude towards Italy and Germany. Although it was an exaggeration, the Nationalists blamed the Soviet Union for the origin and long duration of the Civil War.

With the Nationalist victory, a new regime was installed in Spain, which bore similarities to both Fascist Italy and Nazi Germany. The only political party authorised by the new regime was the Falange. Before the Civil War it had been a minority fascist party, but it had grown massively in the months preceding and during the war. The party members, especially those belonging to the so-called 'Old Guard' (those who had belonged to the Falange before the Civil War) believed Spain was in need of a revolution along the lines of the Italian and German models. They wanted a revolution that would bring both social justice and ambitious economic modernisation. These policies were to be accompanied by nationalist fervour, and put into effect by a dictatorship that would mobilise the masses, especially the country's youth. With these measures, they believed, Spain would again be a great power.

Franco, the head of state and Generalissimo of the Armed Forces, was also head of the Falange. Franco had never been a Falangist, but believed his regime needed an organisation capable of mobilising popular support. However, despite appearances, the Falange had hardly any real power within Spain, which was, in reality, in the hands of institutions like the Armed Forces and the Catholic Church. The most conservative social and economic groups continued to run the country, much to the despair of the Falangists.

The start of World War II saw a pact made between Hitler and Stalin for the carving up of Poland. In Spain, the winners of the Civil War sympathised with Germany, but could not approve under any circumstances of an alliance between the Third Reich and the Soviet Union. The German victory in Poland was not a cause for much celebration in Spain. However, following events in May and June of 1940 when the Wehrmacht crushed France and forced the British to abandon the Continent, the reaction was more enthusiastic. For many Spaniards, France and the United Kingdom were 'historical enemies'. The British occupation of Gibraltar in particular was felt as an affront to national pride.

Following Hitler's victory over France, important sectors of Franco's regime pressured in favour of the country entering the war on the Axis side, while Spain declared itself 'non-belligerent'. Franco, however, was in no hurry. He asked Germany for large supplies of weapons and munitions and the assurance that, following the Axis victory, Spain would recover Gibraltar as well as receiving large tracts of France's African empire. As Germany could not grant these requests, Spain's participation in the war was postponed *sine die*.

The initial batch of volunteers for the division was concentrated in Spanish military barracks in overcrowded conditions. Therefore, it was not uncommon for men to have to eat their meals sitting on the floor. The Spanish Army infantry badge can be seen worn on the collars of the men's blue Falangist shirts (adorned with the yoke and arrows) and on their red berets. (Fundación División Azul, FDA)

The creation of the Blue Division was to lead to a fresh confrontation between the more conservative senior military commanders and the leadership of the Falange; both wanted to control the recruitment process and organisation of the unit. This photograph was taken at one of the barracks where the volunteers were being concentrated. Left, an Army 'provisional' (wartime service commission) lieutenant. Right, a 'jerarca' (political leader) of the Falange. (FDA)

Meanwhile, in Spain the tensions between the different factions that formed the winning side had become acute. The Falangists saw their revolutionary programme forgotten, while other groups represented in Franco's regime – conservatives, Catholics and monarchists – elbowed them out of the power stakes. Furthermore, these factions were also pressuring Franco to cut his ties with the Falange and restore the monarchy. These groups did not view Nazi Germany favourably, considering Hitler's regime to be too dangerously revolutionary for their liking.

For the Falangists, the only possibility that Franco would embark on their political programme rested with the Axis. In a Fascist Europe, Spain would have to follow the same path and carry out the Falangist revolution, and in the 'New Order' that would arise following the Axis victory Spain would be a great power.

When the Wehrmacht attacked the USSR on 22 June 1941, the event was to have a profound impact in Spain. In the days that followed, something happened in Spain that did not even occur in the Third Reich itself: there were large-scale popular demonstrations in the streets of many Spanish towns and cities to celebrate the start of the campaign against communism and to ask that Spanish volunteers be sent. These demonstrations were organised by the Falange, although they were echoed among the people, because the different factions that had supported the Nationalist uprising on 18 July 1936 were unanimously anti-communist.

The Catholic Church had suffered atrociously during the Civil War. Thousands of priests had been assassinated and many thousands of religious buildings had been destroyed. The Vatican had qualified the war against the

Popular Front as a 'Holy Crusade'. Therefore, although the neo-paganism of the Nazis was alarming for Spanish Catholics, it was still considered far preferable to the hatred inspired by the Soviet Union. Other conservative groups in Spain were stupefied to see the United Kingdom ally itself with Stalin. Many of them, who until then would have preferred to see a British victory over Germany, changed their opinion when it became clear that the defeat of Germany would be a victory for Stalin.

So it was that the Blue Division arose with massive popular support from all those social and political groups who had supported the Nationalist Uprising of 18 July 1936. For these sections of Spanish society, the campaign against the Soviet Union was the continuation of a war that had begun in Spain. Therefore, Spain could lay claim to the honour of being 'the first country to defeat communism'. Because of this, it was felt, Spain could not fail to participate in some way in Operation *Barbarossa*.

This desire to fight communism was integral to the origins of the Blue Division and was given as the main justification for its existence. Many of

Volunteers for the Blue Division were given a tremendous send-off. Here, they are seen leaving Barcelona. (FDA)

those who passed through its ranks also wanted to show their sympathy for the Third Reich. They admired its social and economic policies and wished to see similar ideas implanted in Spain. They also hoped that their presence in the campaign in Russia – a campaign it was assumed would end in victory – would result in Spain improving its international position. At the very least, they expected to recover Gibraltar and believed that Spain would extend its possessions in Morocco.

Nevertheless, it was hatred of communism that motivated the majority of the volunteers, which was equally true of those who enlisted in July 1941 and those who did so in the years that followed. In spite of the antipathy that France and the United Kingdom provoked in many Spaniards, there were never any volunteer units formed to fight against the French or British armies. Such a unit was never proposed at any time. After three long years of civil war, the last thing the Spanish people wanted was to become absorbed in another conflict. However, the campaign against communism was something special: it created intense emotion and many Spaniards wished to participate.

Russia had never before been an enemy of Spain, but the Soviet Union was definitely considered an enemy by many Spaniards. Nothing obliged the Spanish to march to Russia to fight communism, but many thousands of them did: some 45,000 took part in that campaign. The profile of the typical soldier filling the ranks of the Blue Division can be perfectly defined from the beginning: volunteer and anticommunist.

A BRIEF CHRONOLOGY

1941

22 June	The start of Operation *Barbarossa*. Two days later, large-scale demonstrations begin in Madrid that soon spread throughout Spain, calling for Spanish volunteers to be sent to join in the campaign against the Soviet Union. The organisation of a volunteer unit is officially begun on the 26th.
13 July	Spanish volunteers start leaving Spain for Germany.
20 August	Following a brief training period at the camp at Grafenwöhr, the Blue Division, designated the 250th Infantry Division of the Heer (German Army), begins its transfer to Poland. The division is composed of three infantry regiments numbered 262, 263 and 269, as well as an artillery regiment, units of sappers, signals, medical staff and other support elements. All these units use the number 250. A small German Liaison Staff is also attached to the divisional headquarters.
27 August	The Blue Division begins its long march on foot to the front, from the Polish-Lithuanian frontier to the area around Smolensk. The original destination of the Blue Division was to be Army Group Centre. However, on 18 September the order was given that it was to join Army Group North.
12 October	The Blue Division starts to deploy on the River Volkhov. Almost simultaneously, the Germans begin operations east of the river, designed to complete the encirclement of Leningrad, liaising with the Finns on the River Svir. With the Wehrmacht at the limit of its strength, the operation succeeds in occupying Tikhvin, but is unable to achieve its

final objective. The Spanish also cross the Volkhov, covering the southernmost flank of the offensive. They become involved in a series of hard-fought engagements, worsened by the horrendously low temperatures, which cause heavy losses in the Blue Division. From 7 December, the Germans initiate their redeployment from Tikhvin back to their starting positions on the Volkhov. The Spanish redeploy to the west of the Volkhov on 7 and 8 December.

23–27 December   The Blue Division repulses heavy Soviet attacks on its sector. These attacks are the preliminary operations of the great offensive the Red Army is about to launch to the north and south of Lake Ilmen. Given the energetic resistance offered by the Spanish troops, the Red Army decides not to attempt a breakthrough in the sector occupied by the Blue Division.

1942

7 January   The Soviets launch their winter offensive against Army Group North. The Russians manage to cross the River Volkhov to north of the sector occupied by the Blue Division, and to the south across Lake Ilmen, and succeed in encircling the Germans in the Demyansk pocket.

10 January   In order to help the Germans south of Lake Ilmen, a company of Spanish ski troops – over 200 men – crosses the lake, with the objective of relieving the garrison in Vsvad. The Spanish company fights south of the lake almost until the end of the month, their numbers finally being reduced to 12 men.

13 January   A Spanish battalion is sent to the aid of the German division deployed north of the Spanish sector in an attempt to contain the Soviet breakthrough on the Volkhov. From this time, and during the following months, different units of the Blue Division are employed as forces attached to German units in different operations designed to stem the Soviet forces crossing the Volkhov.

15 March   The Germans begin operations to encircle the Soviet forces west of the Volkhov, forming the so-called Volkhov Pocket, which is progressively reduced until its final destruction in the middle of June. During the course of this battle, the Blue Division gradually extends its frontline northwards, relieving German units in the process. At the same time, it sends detachments to German formations to participate in the annihilation of the encircled Soviet forces.

6 April   From January to February three march battalions were sent from Spain to cover the large number of Blue Division casualties. From 6 April, the following march battalions were used not only to cover casualties, but mainly to relieve officers, NCOs and soldiers. Up to 30 September 1943, a total of 27 battalions of replacements travelled from Spain to Russia.

24 May   The first battalion of personnel who have been relieved on the Eastern Front after completing their period of service cross the French frontier into Spain. Until this time, only small numbers of wounded men have been repatriated. From this date until October 1943 when the order for the

	disbandment and repatriation of the Blue Division is issued, a total of 13 battalions of men who have completed their service are sent back to Spain.
11 August	Having been assigned to the forces designated for the capture of Leningrad, the Blue Division begins to redeploy from its sector on the Volkhov.
9 September	The Blue Division completes its deployment in the lines encircling Leningrad. However, the planned attack on the city is called off in October. Instead of taking part in a great offensive, the Spanish troops find themselves involved in a hard-fought trench war.
8 November	Operation *Torch* sees Allied troops land in Morocco and Algeria. On the 19th, the Red Army begins operations that will see the annihilation of the Sixth Army in Stalingrad. Given the new international situation, the influence of those who would like to see the Blue Division withdrawn from the Eastern Front grows.
12 December	General Muñoz Grandes hands over command of the Blue Division to General Esteban-Infantes. Muñoz Grandes receives the Knight's Cross with Oak Leaves.

1943

12 January	The Red Army launches Operation *Iskra*, which enables it to establish a corridor south of Ladoga, linking Leningrad to the rest of the Soviet Union. The Blue Division is tasked with relieving those German forces counterattacking the Soviet offensive, dangerously extending its lines.
21 January	A battalion of the Blue Division is detached to the German forces fighting south of Ladoga. In only one week of intense combat, the battalion sees the number of its effectives reduced from 500 to just 30 men.
10 February	The Blue Division comes under heavy attack on its right wing at Krasny Bor. This attack is the first phase of the Red Army's Operation *Polar Star*, which has the ambitious objective of annihilating Army Group North and relieving Leningrad from its encirclement. In spite of the massive deployment of artillery and tanks, and allocating a division for every Spanish battalion that is attacked, the Russian offensive is halted. The Spanish suffer terrible losses (1,000 dead, 200 prisoners and 1,500 wounded) resulting in German forces having to relieve them in the Krasny Bor sector. The Blue Division adjusts its front lines accordingly.
29 July	The US ambassador in Madrid demands that Franco withdraw the Blue Division from Russia. At the end of September, Franco makes the decision to repatriate the Blue Division, but leaves a regiment-sized contingent of volunteers in Russia, who become known as the Blue Legion.
12 October	Army Group North informs the Blue Division that they are to be relieved and repatriated to Spain. Just after the organisation of the Blue Legion begins, General Esteban-Infantes is decorated with the Knight's Cross and then returns to Spain.

| 29 October | The first battalion of effectives from the now disbanded Blue Division crosses the Franco-Spanish frontier. The process is completed on 24 December. |

1944

15 January	The Blue Legion completes its training period and deploys to the front. At the same time, the Red Army launches its offensive to lift the siege of Leningrad and force the Axis forces back into the Baltic States. The Blue Legion, together with the rest of Army Group North, retreats westwards.
20 February	Germany accepts Spain's request for the withdrawal of the Blue Legion.
28 March	Between this date and 12 April, convoys carrying the Blue legion cross the Franco-Spanish frontier.
Spring 1944–May 1945	Small units of Spanish volunteers, recruited by the Germans against the wishes of the Spanish government, normally of company strength, participate at different times and places in the fighting. They fight against communist guerrillas in the south of France, in Slovenia and in northern Italy, against the Red Army in the Carpathian Mountains of Romania, in Pomerania, in Slovakia, and finally, in the battle for Berlin itself. In some cases, these small units form part of the Heer, and in others as part of the Waffen-SS.

RECRUITMENT AND ORGANISATION IN SPAIN (1941–43)

A corporal of the Blue Division's Artillery Regiment arriving at Grafenwöhr. The uniforms issued to the volunteers were modelled on those of the Spanish Army, but were distinct enough to give them the character of a volunteer expeditionary force. The blue shirt and red beret, the symbols of the Falange, underlined the unit's political nature. (FDA)

When the Russian campaign began, the Falange proposed sending a unit of volunteers composed entirely of Falangists. The idea was put forward by Ramón Serrano Suñer, president of the 'Junta Política' (Central Political Committee) of the Falange, who was at the same time also Minister of Foreign Affairs. His objective was twofold: to fight communism, and at the same time to increase the Falange's influence.

During the Civil War, the Falange had organised battalion-strength units of volunteers, called 'Banderas', in which many thousands of men served. However, the regular army made them submit to its authority. Once the war had finished, the Falange tried to create its own permanent armed militia, like the Italian Fascist party's MVSN or the Nazi Party's SS-Verfügungstruppen. Although this Falangist militia was approved, the Spanish Army did everything in its power to prevent it from growing and becoming established, to the extent that it became almost a phantom organisation. When the Falange announced its desire to create the Blue Division as a unit of Falangist militia, the Army reacted immediately: there was no way the Falange would be permitted to have its own military formation.

The Army Minister, General Varela, was markedly opposed to the Falange. He would not accept Serrano's idea and proposed sending a division of regulars. However, this would have implied an official declaration of war against the Soviet Union, so a compromise was reached. The commander, officers and NCOs would be recruited from the Army, as well as specialist troops (such as signals), and soldiers who wished to could also enlist. The rest would be drawn from civilian volunteers recruited through the offices of the Falange's militia.

The Blue Division was organised in Spain in a very short period. Due to massive popular support for the idea, a contingent of 18,000 men was soon raised. Several thousand other aspirants had to content themselves with being placed on a waiting list.

A third of the division's effectives came from the Army: all the officers and NCOs and part of the rank and file (many of these were young Falangists doing their military service). The Falange recruited the remaining two-thirds, although only half of these were party members. Within this group, it is worth noting that a considerable number of them were university students. The University Students' Union (Sindicato de Estudiantes Universitarios, or SEU) was the most radical section of the Falange and was the most supportive of the creation of the Blue Division. Some 4,000 students served with the division, including their national leader.

Convinced as they were that the Blue Division would be significant for the course of domestic politics within Spain following the supposedly imminent German victory, many Falange leaders also signed up to serve in the division.

THE DEPARTURE OF THE BLUE DIVISION

The Blue Division was given a tremendous send-off of the kind never experienced by any other Spanish expeditionary force either before or since. Thousands turned up at the train stations to bid farewell to the men, with many more waving to them as the trains rolled through the stations on their way to the Franco-Spanish frontier. A lieutenant-colonel is shown in the centre foreground, and the collar badges on his uniform and his blue sash show him to be a member of the Staff Corps. He is seen addressing a young provisional (short-service commission) artillery lieutenant, on the far right. As a short-service commission officer, the lieutenant's rank is shown by the two six-pointed stars on the red tab above his left breast, instead of being worn on his cuff. Next to his rank badge is the 1936–39 Campaign Medal. Behind and to the left of the lieutenant-colonel is a Falange 'jerarca' (political leader), bidding farewell to a volunteer, who has pinned a Falange 'yoke and arrows' badge to his tunic as well as revealing the collar of his blue shirt, in order to demonstrate his political militancy. The volunteer also wears a 'detente bala' (bullet stopper) on his uniform, a religious amulet commonly worn during the Spanish Civil War. The amulet, which contained the 'sacred heart of Jesus Christ', was a means of imploring divine protection from enemy fire. On the far left, wearing a grey uniform, is a member of the University Militia, an organisation which formed part of the Falangist University Students' Union (SEU). The University Militia was responsible for the military training of students who would later become reserve officers in the army.

Although neither public opinion nor volunteers for the Blue Division were aware of the fact, the division's creation resulted in an intense political battle between the Falange's leaders and the military high command. The former believed that Spain should undergo a political revolution according to Falangist ideals, whereas the military affirmed that communism in Spain had been defeated by the army, not a fascist political movement (such as that in Italy and Germany). The Falange had only been a collaborating political force and could not, therefore, aspire to total political control. As a result, the Falange and the army had different visions for the expeditionary force. The army always designated the unit as the DEV ('Division Española de Voluntarios', Spanish Volunteer Division) and this was its official name. However, the Blue Division has always been the commonly used name. In reality, if it had not been for the Falange, the unit would never have existed, and of all the volunteers that passed through its ranks, the most important contingent were the members of the Falange.

Those civilian volunteers who were not Falangists in the strictest sense, but rather conservatives, monarchists, Catholics, etc., were certainly no less anti-communist. Although the division was officially named the Spanish Volunteer Division, given the high proportion of Falangists within its ranks, it soon became known as the Blue Division – blue being the colour of the shirts worn by the Falange.

General Muñoz Grandes was chosen to lead the division. He was an officer of great prestige and at the same time one of the few Spanish general officers known to support the Falange. His appointment was acceptable, therefore, to both the Falange and the Army.

The almost universal belief that the campaign in Russia would be another victorious German blitzkrieg operation soon evaporated following the German defeat at the gates of Moscow. The Blue Division, like any other unit of the Wehrmacht, suffered heavy losses during the operations from the autumn of 1941 to the winter of early 1942. News of the terrible losses and horrendous conditions on the Eastern Front (especially the cold) soon reached Spain. Even so, when the time came to call on those volunteers who had been unable to find a place in the division in July 1941 to come forward and replace the casualties, the majority of them did so.

However, the recruitment process was by this time completely in the hands of the Army, who made sure that the majority of new recruits came from their own ranks, reducing enlistment by Falangists to a minimum. The Army minister, Varela, supported the idea of substituting the 'first division', which had been predominantly Falangist, for a 'second division', which would be almost purely military. For his part, the Falange leader, Serrano, was conscious of the fact that a massive enlistment of Falangists would turn against him as the campaign in Russia dragged on without a German victory. While thousands of Falangists were fighting in Russia (many dying in the process), the most reactionary elements in Franco's regime had been quick to occupy their vacant positions and so the Falange, instead of increasing its political power in Spain, was in fact losing influence. The party therefore requested that the main leaders serving with the Blue Division in Russia be returned to Spain, and at the same time tried to make sure that in the future there would be no massive exodus of Falangists to the Eastern Front.

The profile of the typical volunteer had begun to change by the middle of 1942. The Blue Division had always had a large number of Falangists in its ranks, but the percentage of recruits coming from the Army and civilians with no connections to the Falange began to increase steadily. However, the vast majority of these volunteers continued to have strong anti-communist sentiments. It should be pointed out that the Falangists were not the only group in Spain who were fervently anti-communist. The Popular Front had murdered thousands of non-Falangists, many being devoted Catholics,

General Muñoz Grandes with his six colonels in a photo taken in Grafenwöhr. Colonel Rodrigo, on the general's right, wears the San Fernando Cross, the most prestigious Spanish decoration. He was the division's second-in-command. The others commanded the three infantry regiments, the artillery regiment and the staff. (FDA).

Spanish NCOs working at the Blue Division headquarters. In contrast to the Heer, the Spanish Army did not have numerous and well-trained NCOs. (FDA)

landowners, businessmen and from other sectors of society. Many of the relatives of these victims had as strong a desire to put an end to communism as the Falangists.

What is true is that while the volunteers who came forward in 1941 did so on the wave of popular enthusiasm for the cause (following large-scale demonstrations and a huge press campaign), by 1942, and even more so in 1943, the situation had become distinct. The newer volunteers came in dribs and drabs, enlisting at army barracks or in the offices of the Falange's militia.

The wave of excitement for the crusade against communism that accompanied enlistment in 1941, and which defined the early volunteers for the original Blue Division, would not be repeated. Contrary to the idealism that filled the first expedition of 1941, it was now common to find many recruits who had enlisted with other priorities foremost in their minds, such as the pay, the possibilities for rapid promotion in the case of officers and

NCOs, or a reduction in the period of military service. There were, in fact, a combination of factors that had not been an influence in the decision to join up in 1941, when the immense majority of the volunteers had enlisted before knowing what the conditions of service and pay would be.

However, it is also true to say that, unlike those who had joined in 1941, the volunteers who came forward to serve on the Eastern Front in 1942 and 1943 were well aware of what they were letting themselves in for; none of them believed they were in for an easy time. The many men who had returned to Spain mutilated, suffering the effects of frostbite and weary of the horrors of war had recounted the terrible nature of the Eastern Front. Every day, the Spanish newspapers published the names and details of those men who had perished in Russia. Nevertheless, volunteers continued to come forward, although in ever fewer numbers as time went on.

In August 1942, due to an internal political crisis in Franco's regime, both General Varela and Serrano lost their posts. The new Army minister, the Germanophile General Asensio, wanted to boost the Blue Division, as he continued to believe in a final German victory. Once Serrano had fallen from power, leadership of the Falange passed into the hands of José Luis de Arrese. He also wanted to increase the contribution of the Blue Division. However, the new Minister of Foreign Affairs, Gómez-Jordana (also a general in the Army) no longer believed a German victory was possible now that the United States had entered the conflict. Gómez-Jordana wanted Spain to break its ties with the Third Reich, abandon its status as a 'non-belligerent', and take up the posture of a neutral country. He was particularly worried about the

This was one of the many postcards produced by German propaganda for distribution among the Spanish troops. It shows General Moscardó, the legendary hero of the defence of the 'Alcázar de Toledo' during his visit to the Blue Division. He is greeting one of the division's most prominent Falangists, Sergeant Luis Nieto, who, years later, was to become President of the Blue Division Veterans' Association. In the centre is General Muñoz Grandes, wearing his characteristic, though wholly anti-regulation, yellow scarf. (FDA)

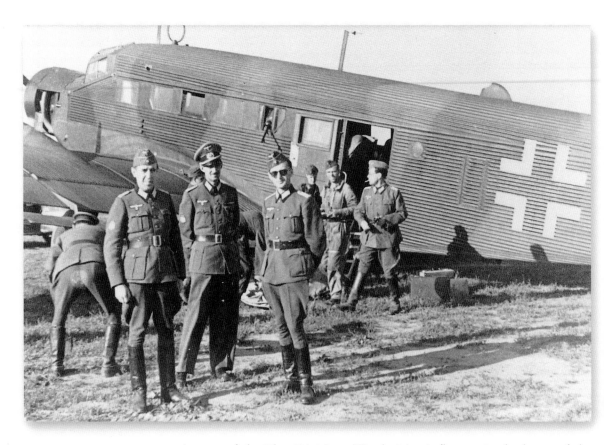

From spring 1942 onwards, one Junkers Ju-52 linked Berlin, the airbase where the Blue Squadron was deployed (in Central Russia) and the Blue Division headquarters by means of a weekly triangular trip. The aircraft was a Spanish Ju-52, although it used Luftwaffe markings. This made possible rapid travelling from the front to Berlin and from there to Madrid. This route was used by high-ranking officers and to send very important documents. (FDA)

existence of the Blue Division. His decisive influence in the heart of the Spanish government ensured that no new propaganda campaigns were allowed in order to recruit volunteers for the Blue Division.

The international situation also contributed to reducing the number of volunteers. When the Allies landed in North Africa in November 1942, American troops were deployed in Morocco facing Spanish positions in that country. Many believed that an attack would be launched on Franco's Spain. The Spanish Army reacted by calling up new drafts and activating reservists. For many, to continue to maintain a Spanish division in Russia, given the circumstances, was absurd, especially when one considers that the threat of an Allied invasion of Spain appeared very real.

Finally, it is necessary to bear in mind that although the Blue Division had popular support from its inception to disbandment, the Spanish people did not want to be involved in World War II. In July 1941, when it was believed the Soviet Union would be quickly defeated and the United Status had not yet entered the war, the Blue Division did not present a high risk that Spain would be dragged into the conflict. From December 1941 onwards, the international situation changed. Even markedly anti-communist elements in the regime began to consider that the Blue Division posed a decided risk.

The invasion of Sicily, which brought about the fall of Mussolini's regime, set off all the alarms in Spain. General Gómez-Jordana, Minister of Foreign Affairs, saw his predictions on the risks implicit in Spain's continued relations with Nazi Germany becoming more real. He attempted to veto the enlistment of any more volunteers and obtain the quick repatriation of the Blue Division, which he achieved in October 1943. In order to ease things with the Germans he agreed to leave the Blue Legion on the Eastern Front (a much smaller unit consisting of only two battalions of infantry and a mixed battalion of combat support elements including artillery, anti-tank units, etc.). Just a few months later this formation was also disbanded. By then the Germans had already begun the clandestine recruitment of Spanish volunteers to be integrated into German units (although in far smaller numbers than those of 1941). However, there were several hundred Spanish volunteers ready to continue the fight against communism to the end, and in fact, a few of them even fought in the battle for Berlin in 1945.

TRAINING IN GERMANY

The Germans allocated a substantial period of time for training their troops before sending them to the front, and therefore intended to do the same with the Blue Division. However, in the summer of 1941 the Wehrmacht achieved spectacular victories against the Red Army and the Spanish feared that by the time the Blue Division was ready to march to the front the war would be over. General Muñoz Grandes persuaded the Germans to authorise a greatly reduced training programme, less than a month in fact, arguing that all his men were veterans of the Civil War and therefore had military experience.

In reality, only the officers and NCOs were all veterans of the Civil War; the majority of the volunteers enlisted in the Blue Division had not been able to fight the 'Reds' in Spain and this had been precisely one of the reasons many had joined up. Some had been imprisoned by the Popular Front, others had not been old enough to fight, while others had been trapped in areas of the country controlled by the government and had been forced to join the ranks of the Spanish Republican Army. Therefore, they now wished to do what they could not do during the Civil War: fight communism.

Two fallen soldiers, one Spanish and one German, about to be buried in a military cemetery full of Spanish graves. The Spanish coffin is covered with the Spanish flag, and the German one with the Reichskriegsflagge. The cortège is headed by a Spanish military chaplain. Five thousand men of the division lost their lives during the campaign. For the German soldiers, this was the most clear example of Spanish–German 'Waffenbruderschaft'. (FDA)

The Blue Division had a highly select officer corps. This captain wears the insignia for 'military academy professors' over his left breast. (FDA)

The Germans were very familiar with the Spanish Army, having deployed their Condor Legion in Spain. They were aware that the Spanish Army had always modelled itself along the lines of the French Army, which they had so convincingly crushed in 1940. In the eyes of the Germans, in terms of its tactics and training, the Spanish Army was very deficient, but they accepted Muñoz Grandes' proposition because they believed that the Blue Division would have to make no more than a symbolic contribution to the campaign.

On the other hand, the Spanish volunteers showed themselves to be good students and soon learned to handle German equipment and weapons. The reasons for this were twofold: first of all, they were enthusiastic volunteers, and secondly, a high proportion of them were university students, who brought their intellectual and academic qualities with them. In other circumstances, these men would have been chosen to become Reserve Junior Officers, but in the Blue Division they made up the rank and file.

The period of training, therefore, was very brief. On several occasions, the German commanders of the army corps in which the Blue Division was to be integrated, lamented that the division had not been trained to the same criteria and for the same length of time as a German division.

This problem had not been solved when battalions of replacements began arriving from Spain. Once in Germany, they were equipped, sworn in and were sent off to the front at the earliest opportunity.

COMPOSITION

One of the unique aspects of the Blue Division, in comparison with other military units in contemporary Spanish military history, is that of having had a cadre of officers of the highest quality. Some 2,400 Spanish officers served with the division (from second lieutenants to colonels) and of these more than 300 finished their military careers with the rank of general.

Before the Civil War, officers in the Spanish Army were divided between those who had left-wing sympathies (a minority) and those who leaned towards the right (the majority). However, the army that emerged from the conflict was overwhelmingly anti-communist.

The best officers tended to choose posts commanding Spanish troops in North Africa: the Spanish Legion (inspired by the French Foreign Legion) or the 'Regulares' (composed of both Spanish and native Moroccan troops). The Blue Division soon earned the same level of prestige as the Spanish Legion and the 'Regulares'. In fact, many of those officers who served with the Blue Division came from the Spanish Legion and 'Regulares'.

The most deplorable characteristic of the Spanish officer corps was a common feature in armies of the period, that of class division. Officers considered themselves a caste apart from the NCOs and soldiers. All of them had soldiers to act as their batmen and required mess and accommodation facilities in conditions superior to the rest of the men. Even the beating of soldiers was not viewed as unacceptable behaviour. These pitiful defects became more apparent when the troops of the Blue Division compared their officers with those of the Wehrmacht. Spanish soldiers, for example, were greatly surprised to see that, during mealtimes in the messes they used during their transfer, German officers, even generals, waited their turn in the queues, alongside simple soldiers, without expecting privilege due to their rank.

Generals and field officers

The Blue Division was commanded successively by generals Agustín Muñoz Grandes (from August 1941 to 12 December 1942), Emilio Esteban-Infantes Martín (to 20 October 1943) and Santiago Amado Lóriga (to December 1943, when the division was officially disbanded).

Muñoz Grandes was the division's most outstanding commander. He came from a family with no military tradition and had commanded colonial troops in Morocco, where he had been wounded at least eight times. Muñoz Grandes was one of the most respected officers in the Spanish Army. Unlike most of his colleagues, he did not sympathise with the monarchy when the Republic was installed in Spain, and the government tasked him with organising an elite police corps. However, his religious convictions and deeply felt patriotism prevented him from collaborating with the Popular Front. Following the success of the Popular Front, he gravitated towards the Falange. When the Nationalist Uprising occurred, he was detained and condemned to death. Following several anxious months spent in prison, his former police subordinates managed to

The soldiers of the Blue Division constantly displayed their Falangist affiliation. This particular example appeared at the entrance to the division's general headquarters. (FDA)

Falangist symbols displayed on Heer uniforms. The soldier in the centre is wearing the emblem of the SEU (University Students' Union) and the man to his right displays the badge of the Falange Youth Organisation. Both organisations formed part of the Falange's 'Frente de Juventudes' (Youth Front). (FDA)

rescue him and transfer him to the Nationalist zone. Once there, he quickly rose to command an army corps. When the war was over, given that he was one of the few generals sympathetic to the Falange, he was appointed secretary general of the organisation. However, he soon resigned, as he had no liking for the world of politics. He was then appointed to command the Spanish troops deployed around Gibraltar. If Spanish plans drawn up in 1940 to attack the British base had been put into effect, he would have commanded the operation. He was, in short, one of the most capable Spanish generals at that time.

The most noticeable quality about Muñoz Grandes was his charisma among his soldiers. Those who served under his orders in Russia idolised him. The general treated them with a paternal attitude and was always concerned to make sure that their living conditions were the best available. To this effect, he frequently paid surprise visits to the frontline. On a personal level he was austere and of an extraordinary sobriety. He never wore his numerous decorations on his uniform and nor did he wear the coat of a German Army general with its conspicuous red facing, preferring that of a common soldier. Just like his men, he paid little attention to the rigid German regulations regarding uniforms and was always seen out and about wearing a yellow scarf wrapped around his neck, as well as a cigarette hanging from his bottom lip. Thanks to the devotion of his men, Muñoz Grandes was able to ask them to make all manner of sacrifices, confident that they would do all that was possible to obey his orders.

Muñoz Grandes was a firm supporter of Nazi Germany. He believed that Hitler's regime had developed the social and economic policies that were needed in Spain. Moreover, he believed the alliance between Spain and Germany would allow Spain to become a great power. He was committed to the idea of Spanish expansion in Africa.

The Germans also soon learned to appreciate him, realising that he was the heart and soul of the Blue Division. He especially enjoyed the favour of Hitler, who despised Franco and hoped that Muñoz Grandes would succeed him as the head of the Spanish government. Muñoz Grandes was awarded the Knight's Cross with Oak Leaves.

Following World War II, Muñoz Grandes went on to occupy important military and political positions in Spain. Within the context of the Cold War, he was responsible on the Spanish side for organising military collaboration with the United States. In spite of the fact that in his day he had been categorised as 'Hitler's Spanish general', he was received by all the important authorities in Washington and was even awarded American decorations.

When from April 1942, General Varela was attempting to substitute the Falangist 'First Division' for a purely military 'Second Division', he appointed General Esteban-Infantes as commander. Esteban-Infantes came from a traditional military family and had been active in the monarchist cause and implicated in the attempted *coup d'état* against the Republican government in 1932 and was detained and thrown out of the army. He joined the Nationalist Army during the Civil War and commanded important formations. He was, however, a typical staff officer, spending his time in his office and rarely visiting the frontline. His manner was aloof, distant, and he never succeeded in acquiring the same devotion from his men as Muñoz Grandes.

The first winter was to prove extremely arduous for the Spanish. To help against the cold the volunteers received a balaclava from Spain. This headwear had been manufactured during the Civil War for distribution among the International Brigades. No other unit in the Heer wore this head garment. There can be no mistaking the nationality of this particular volunteer, who has pinned the Falangist 'yoke and arrows' to the front of his balaclava. (FDA)

Esteban-Infantes should have relieved Muñoz Grandes as commander in June 1942, but the latter refused to return to Spain and knew he could count on the support of the Germans. Therefore, Esteban-Infantes had to settle for being second-in-command of the division until December 1942. During his period of command, the Blue Division fought the hardest battle in its history, at Krasny Bor. The Germans never held Esteban-Infantes in the same esteem as Muñoz Grandes.

Following the end of World War II, Esteban-Infantes also occupied important military posts in Spain and, in fact, it was he who was most concerned for the welfare of the Blue Division's veterans. The austere and morally incorruptible Muñoz Grandes never allowed his veterans to enjoy any special privileges for being ex-combatants, whereas Esteban-Infantes helped many of the veterans to gain employment, housing and other privileges. He attended the veterans' meetings and wrote the first history of the Blue Division to honour his former soldiers.

The division's last commander, General Amado, had joined the unit as a colonel commanding a regiment, and received his promotion while in Russia. As commander-in-chief of the Blue Division, his only task was to supervise its repatriation.

The regimental and battalion commanders had been chosen by Muñoz Grandes (in July 1941) and later by Esteban-Infantes (when what became known as the 'Second Division' was being organised). In both cases, they chose those they considered to be men like themselves. Muñoz Grandes selected veterans of the campaigns in Africa, accustomed to commanding legionaries (most of whom came from society's lowest orders, real 'desperados' in many cases) and ferocious Moroccan tribesmen. These officers were very doubtful of the effectiveness of a division composed mainly of students and did not

DECORATIONS AND BADGES

The Spanish volunteers wore their own decorations and badges on their German uniforms, and in this way made them to a certain degree more 'Spanish'. **(1)** Individual Military Medal, **(2)** San Fernando Cross and **(3)** War Cross, **(4)** Red Cross and **(5)** the Medal for Wounds received in the Service of the Nation. Many Spanish volunteers wore these awards on their German uniforms, having been awarded them during the Spanish Civil War. All of these decorations were also awarded to members of the Blue Division during the Russian campaign. **(6)** 1936–39 Campaign Medal (awarded to all veterans of the Nationalist Army). **(7)** Falange 'Old Guard' medal (for those who had been members before the Civil War).
(8) The most common Falange 'yoke and arrows' badge (non-regulation), which appeared in several variants (both metal and cloth) and sizes. It was worn on the breast, on the sleeves and headgear, according to the wearer's taste. **(9)** Ranks within the Falange and its subordinate organisations were identified by stars, yokes and arrows, which were of different colours (gold, silver, red and green). Many Falangists who served in the Blue Division, wore these insignia on their German uniforms.
(10) Still more common was the wearing of the SEU insignia: a swan on blue and white chequering. The colour of the swan varied and this represented the rank of the wearer. **(11)** In contrast, the circular emblem of the Falange Youth Organisation only ever appeared in the design shown in this illustration.
Insignia typical of the Spanish Army appeared on the uniforms worn from Spain to the base at Hof, in Germany, and on the return journey. More unusually, but on occasion, some of these insignia also appeared on the 'Feldgrau' uniform. **(12)** Heraldic symbol of the Spanish Army, **(13)** infantry, **(14)** artillery and **(15)** engineers (including sappers and signals) and **(16)** the Spanish Legion. **(17)** The medal commemorating the Russian campaign, created by the government for volunteers of the Blue Division. **(18)** Cross of the Order of the German Eagle, awarded by the Third Reich to foreigners, and worn by many members of the Blue Division from private soldiers to officers, and by important political figures in Spain. **(19)** The Wehrmacht had a commemorative medal struck especially for Spanish volunteers – an exceptional case, as there was no similar decoration for other units of foreign volunteers. **(20)** The national shield, in the colours of the Spanish flag with 'España', provided by the Wehrmacht, was frequently substituted by Spanish troops with homemade articles. Therefore, several variants existed **(21)**. The most common were adorned with yokes and arrows and iron crosses.

A Provisional Infantry 2nd Lieutenant belonging to one of the first march battalions, on his way to Germany. Many of these junior officers were also members of the Falange, which enabled them to easily forge ties of camaraderie with the men under their command. (FDA)

know how to deal with such soldiers, which in turn made relations with their men quite difficult at first. Neither were these officers sympathetic to troops unaccustomed to the fierce discipline of the Spanish Legion. However, once the campaign had begun and the young Falangists had shown themselves to be no worse soldiers than the legionaries, but rather the opposite, the tension disappeared and the soldiers realised that their veteran officers were the best leaders they could have in the battles that followed.

The officers selected by Esteban-Infantes in many cases had better academic military training and many were also veterans of Africa. However, for some of them the hard conditions of the campaign in Russia proved to be beyond their capabilities and they had to be relieved.

Many battalion commanders achieved tremendous popularity with their men and transformed their battalions into elite units within the division. Revealingly, these proved to be men who even before the Civil War had already been involved with the Falange. The most famous of these was Major Miguel Román Garrido, an officer from the 'Regulares', who thanks to his activity with the Falangists achieved an easy rapport with his men. His battalion, the II./269, took a notable part in all the actions involving the Blue Division and suffered more casualties than any other battalion in the division.

Junior officers

While almost all the regimental and battalion commanders in the Blue Division were professionals who had begun their careers before the Civil War, the situation concerning junior officers was quite the reverse. One of the first decisions taken by the Spanish Republic was the closure of the General Military Academy (the equivalent of Sandhurst or West Point), which in turn resulted in a sharp downturn in the number of officers with such a background of preparation, while the Civil War saw the death of many of those that did. In order to cover the vacant posts, the Nationalist Army had created a Provisional Officer Corps that, initially, was only to exist for the duration of the war. Thousands of university students received wartime commissions as 'Alféreces Provisionales' (provisional second lieutenants). Those who exhibited the necessary qualities were promoted to 'provisional lieutenants and captains'. Once the war had finished, most returned to their studies or civil occupations, but others had discovered their military vocation and wished to continue in the army. To this end, the army organised 'conversion academies' where these wartime officers could complete their training, as what they had received during the conflict had been superficial. This process of conversion had not been completed when recruitment began for the Blue Division. The cadets at these academies volunteered for the division practically en masse. The army filled the posts of lieutenants and second lieutenants with those who were still 'provisionals'. There were so many applications that many, unable to get a post as an officer, enlisted as common soldiers in the offices of the Falange militia.

For these junior officers, the idea of serving alongside the Wehrmacht, then reputed to be the best in the world, seemed the ideal way to complete their military training. There was a strong desire to show that they could be as good at soldiering as the Germans, and so they went to Russia with the objective of absorbing the most advanced military techniques.

Unlike the field officers, the majority of these company officers were capable of establishing excellent relations with the men under their command. These men were not part of the traditional military officer caste and, before the Civil War, many had been sympathisers or members of the Falange. As a result, if the majority of the volunteers felt the relationship with their field officers to be cold and distant, they felt strong links of camaraderie with their company officers (a camaraderie that would continue after the campaign had finished). The feeling was mutual; many company officers who served in the Blue Division were later to write in their memoirs that throughout their careers (which were lengthy in many cases) they never had under their command soldiers as good as those with whom they had served in Russia.

Those field officers who served on the Eastern Front also expressed this same point of view. Professional soldiers as ideologically distant from the Falange as General Esteban-Infantes, Colonel José Martínez Esparza (first commander of the 269th Regiment) or Lieutenant Colonel José Díaz de Villegas (an officer who served on the division's staff), wrote books on the campaign in Russia. All were unanimous in their praise for the soldierly qualities of the civilian Falangists who composed the bulk of the Blue Division.

Muñoz Grandes bids farewell to veterans forming the first battalion to be repatriated to Spain. The popularity he enjoyed among his men is easily visible. (FDA)

José Miguel Guitarte, national leader of the SEU, at the start of the return journey to Spain. He wears the Silver Palm on his left sleeve, the highest decoration awarded by the Falange, which he received for his participation in street battles against the 'Reds' in Spain. Before joining the Falange, he had been a member of the Spanish Young Communists. He served as a private in the Blue Division and was awarded the Iron Cross 2nd Class. Guitarte died soon after returning to Spain from an illness he had contracted on the Russian Front. (FDA)

NCOs

It is without doubt that the main difference between the Spanish Army and the Wehrmacht was in the role played by the NCOs. The Spanish Army was very similar to most European armies of the time in which the NCOs were not trained at academies. Generally, they were long-service soldiers with little or no academic background. It would not be unusual to find that many had stayed in the army for no other reason than to have regular meals and a roof over their heads. They were held in contempt by the officers and hated by the men.

During the Civil War, thousands of men had been appointed 'provisional sergeants'. After the conflict had been concluded, while the Spanish Army made a serious effort to convert its wartime commissioned officers into good professionals, it did not pay the same attention to its so-called 'provisional NCOs' who, in many cases, wished to continue in the army, but had to accept 'demotion' to the rank of corporal, which frustrated many of them.

This lack of consideration towards its NCOs led to a revealing situation. For each place available in the division for a soldier in July 1941 there were four or five volunteers, but for officers it was even higher, with almost 10 applicants for each post. However, in the case of NCOs, the army had difficulty in finding enough men to cover all the posts.

The lack of NCOs became even more noticeable when the Blue Division adopted the German establishment in which NCOs were more numerous than in Spanish units, and had functions that had never been assigned to them in Spain. For Spanish NCOs of the Blue Division, to see the respect given to their German counterparts by both officers and men was a cause for envy.

The NCOs of the Blue Division also had to deal with two other specific problems. Firstly, many of the men under their command were better educated than themselves, which made it difficult for them to command these students or graduates and made their own lack of education more evident.

The other problem appeared when the Blue Division began the policy of relieving men who had spent many months at the front. This was quite easy to do when it came to soldiers and officers, but became very difficult in the case of NCOs, as there were never enough of their comrades back in Spain willing to relieve them.

The volunteers: from university teachers to peasants

It has already been mentioned that the initial recruitment for the Blue Division produced an extraordinary phenomenon in which thousands of university and high school students answered the call for volunteers. University professors also enlisted, although in far fewer numbers, and were accompanied by doctors, journalists, politicians and young writers. There is no doubt that no Spanish unit, either before or since, could count on having so many men of such educational and intellectual background filling its ranks.

However, the Blue Division was not exclusively made up of the kind of men previously mentioned. Volunteers largely drawn from the urban middle classes dominated the first contingent. The Spanish proletariat had supported the Popular Front and so its presence in the ranks of the Blue Division was very much reduced, although there was no shortage of industrial workers within its ranks.

Spain was essentially an agricultural country in 1941, with most of its population living in the countryside. The rural population was politically divided and in some regions, as a consequence of poverty, there were those who had sympathised with the Popular Front. But in those regions where conditions were better, people were generally very conservative and strongly opposed to all those who wished to introduce the collectivisation of land. They were also deeply religious; in few words, they were profoundly anti-communist.

When the division was being quickly organised in 1941, urban inhabitants – who were nearest to the recruitment offices – took the majority of the available places. However, the situation changed in 1942 and 1943. By this time, the enthusiasm for the campaign had dampened down once the truth regarding the terrible conditions on the Eastern Front had begun to filter back. Nevertheless, the mass of rural inhabitants, especially those in Castile and Galicia, which were very conservative regions, continued to be a source of recruits. For many of these men, the first time they had been away from their villages was when they had been called up for military service, and, given the situation, many opted to march to Russia. The social make-up of the Blue Division was therefore being modified. From its initial atypical composition, it evolved into a formation that better reflected the sociological reality of Spain at that time: that of an agrarian nation.

The most remarkable aspect of the second phase of the Blue Division's history was the high percentage of men from those Spanish troops stationed in Morocco, especially legionaries. Being professional soldiers, these men tended to hold firmly patriotic beliefs, but their psychology, origins and mode of behaviour were far from those of the 'falangistas' of the first contingent of volunteers.

Nearly all the volunteers sent their families photographs like this example, which showed them dressed in the uniform of the Heer. (FDA)

However, this surprising mixture of Falangist students, legionaries and peasants worked well. The first, motivated by their political fanaticism, proved themselves excellent fighters. Since the creation of the Spanish Legion, its members had been in the vanguard of the Spanish Army, and so they were in Russia. As far as the latter group was concerned, they were like countrymen all over the world, excellent potential soldiers. Hardened by working outdoors, respectful of the established hierarchy, frugal and austere, the peasants were easily converted into frontline soldiers.

Veterans of the Blue Division have written many books over the years describing their experiences in Russia. The majority of them belonged to the students of the first contingent. The image created of the Blue Division soldier is essentially that of these men. But it must not be forgotten that the ranks of the Blue Division were filled with volunteers from many backgrounds.

A Spanish volunteer wearing a 'Zeltbahn' (winter cape). The Blue Division also received a small number of 'Tarnjacke' (the lightweight army camouflage smock). However, the division's overall use of camouflaged garments was limited. (FDA)

TACTICS

Like many other European armies of the period, the Spanish admired that which was held to be the best in Europe: the French Army, whose doctrines it followed. German tactical ideas on the 'war of movement', especially the concept of blitzkrieg, were far from Spanish military thinking. As Spain was not a heavily industrialised country, it could not even begin to dream of conducting a motorised and armoured war. For similar reasons, the German 'Auftragtaktik' was also beyond Spanish military doctrine. The short time given over to training the Blue Division in Germany could not change this situation.

When the Blue Division crossed the Volkhov in October 1941, it began to operate along those established lines habitual in the Spanish Army (inspired by French tactics): an advance, which in German eyes was too slow and too preoccupied with protecting the flanks. However, the sudden halting of the Blue Division's attack was not due to the tactical limitations of the Spanish, but rather the fact that the Germans halted the attack in the division's sector, in order to concentrate their forces for the attack on Tikhvin and towards the River Svir. Therefore, the Blue Division went on the defensive, holding fixed positions.

Again, the Spanish relied on French tradition – a rigid defence as opposed to the flexible defence favoured by the Germans, which enabled them to take maximum advantage of their superiority in tactical manoeuvre. This was just the moment in which the Red Army launched its winter offensive and Hitler demanded to his forces to hold at all costs. The Blue Division was able to operate perfectly well in this new situation.

The Spanish Division's weaknesses in the war of movement again became apparent when some of its units joined the operation against the Soviet forces in the Volkhov Pocket, during the spring and summer of 1942. The Germans specifically referred to the difficulty in synchronising their attacks with the Spanish. There was also a practical difficulty here in the presence of

A group of Spanish volunteers attempt to keep warm. Although the climatic conditions were adverse, the volunteers managed to overcome them. (FDA)

the language barrier between the Spanish and German forces. On the Leningrad front, where the fighting was static, the problem disappeared. The Spanish troops fought magnificently in this type of warfare.

However, from the German point of view, the rigid form of defence practised by the Spanish led them to incur higher casualties than were necessary. According to the Germans, the Spanish compensated for their lack of tactical expertise with courage and, in a sense, they were right. The Spanish Legion, which represented the elite in Spanish fighting units, cultivated valour of an almost suicidal nature and their battle cry was 'Viva la Muerte!' (which translates, rather paradoxically, as 'Long live Death!'). For their part, the Falangists, like all fascist movements, had made the cult of

A Russian hamlet in the Blue Division's rearguard. The humble wooden houses, called 'isbas', were the preferred accommodation of the volunteers, rather than the underground bunkers. The Spanish custom of putting their hands in their pockets annoyed the Germans greatly. (FDA)

their fallen comrades the most important part of their rituals. For them, sacrificing one's life in combat was the highest form of valour. This peculiar ethos led the Spanish troops to show great contempt for enemy fire.

To the desperation of the Germans, the Spanish used their bugles to issue orders in the frontline, or broke into rousing choruses of Falangist hymns at the start of their assaults on the enemy positions. Instead of using the cover of the trenches, the Spanish would move about the frontline outside of them, unnecessarily exposing themselves to enemy fire. Some of the Spanish officers took time to analyse the main causes of casualties in their units; significantly, the greatest percentage were due to enemy mortar fire, which was attributed to the fact that the Spanish troops considered it unmanly to seek shelter from this kind of projectile.

One veteran narrates the following anecdote, which occurred when his unit was relieving a German unit. Off-duty Spanish troops had gathered to look at the Germans. At that moment the characteristic whistle of incoming artillery rounds was heard. The German officer ordered all his men to take cover, which they did. The Spanish troops, who were veterans, had calculated that the projectiles would land some distance away and so remained on their feet. They then laughed at the Germans, referring to them as 'green'. Much to their surprise, when the German officer got up, the Spanish soldiers saw that his uniform was covered in decorations, as were those of many of his men. A few days later, this same group of Spaniards were taking advantage of a few hours of sunshine to relax outside the narrow trenches. The sound of enemy projectiles was again heard whistling over their heads, but the men ignored them, until a mortar bomb fell short and exploded amongst the group of soldiers, killing several of them. The veteran ended by recognising that the German precautions were correct. The story reveals very well the different attitude exhibited by the Spanish and Germans. For the former, war was basically a question of courage. For the latter, it was about technique with corresponding rules to be followed.

The Blue Division found itself in the same situation on the Eastern Front as the armies of Germany's other allies in the theatre, the Romanians, Italians and Hungarians – experiencing difficulty in trying to keep up with a military machine as effective as the Wehrmacht. However, unlike the armies of these three nations, the Blue Division never collapsed under the weight of a Soviet offensive. This was clearly not the result of some 'innate superiority' of the Spanish as soldiers. Rather, the reason can be found in the fact that the Romanian, Italian and Hungarian armies fought on the Eastern Front with conscripts who for the most part had no ideological motivation, whereas the Blue Division was composed of volunteers who were very well aware of the significance of their presence in Russia.

It should also be pointed out that while the Blue Division never managed to completely absorb German tactical doctrine, the division had been equipped with German weapons, which was another notable difference when compared with the Romanians, Italians and Hungarians.

In spite of tactical limitations, the Germans maintained the Blue Division in the front line, the only exception being the time taken to transfer the division from the Volkhov Pocket to the Leningrad front. The Blue Division was never sent to the rear to rest and always remained at the front to cover relatively wide and sensitive areas. Unlike many of the formations pertaining to the armies of the German allies or foreign volunteer units, the Blue Division was never withdrawn from the frontline to participate in anti-partisan operations. All this means that the Germans obviously had confidence in the division's combat capability.

Paella is one of the most typical of Spanish dishes. Even in Russia, the troops could not do without it. (FDA)

LIFE ON THE EASTERN FRONT

Mud and cold

Although no national insignia is visible, it is clear this man is a Spaniard. He is seen drinking red wine from a 'bota'. (FDA)

Most Europeans think of Spain as a land of beaches and sunshine. However, in reality, in some regions of the country the winters can be quite cold. Nevertheless, the climatic conditions that were to confront the volunteers of the Blue Division in Russia were far worse than those normally experienced in Spain. For the Spanish soldiers, the thought of spending weeks without even seeing the sun was inconceivable and depressing.

The season of 'rasputitsa', the Russian mud, in which movement was rendered almost impossible, was the first big surprise. When the Spanish crossed the Volkhov in the middle of October 1942, the 'rasputitsa' was still present and the problems it posed contributed to halting the Blue Division's advance. All the vehicles, from trucks to bicycles, became useless.

During the operations against the Soviet troops trapped in the Volkhov Pocket, the Spanish troops had to operate in an environment that was wholly new to them: the thick, swampy forests of northern Russia. They had to advance knee-deep in water through forests of a size and density completely unknown in Spain, all the while tormented by clouds of mosquitoes.

However, the worst problem was undoubtedly the freezing cold and snow. Before the Blue Division had even reached the frontline, the men were already succumbing to the effects of the intense cold. When the first snow fell at the beginning of October, the troops could not shake off their astonishment. The very low temperatures at the end of 1941 and beginning of 1942 proved to be a terrible experience for the Spanish soldiers. Both the Germans and Russians physically suffered from the low temperatures like the Spanish, but the major difference was at the psychological level. For the Spanish, it was simply a shock that such low temperatures could exist and many of the volunteers suffered more because they had never even seen snow before and suddenly found themselves in the middle of a campaign being fought in arctic conditions. For these men this was to be a totally new experience. It was no coincidence that the best medical handbook available in Spain during the

Muñoz Grandes surrounded by his officers. At the far left of the standing row is Major Tomás García Rebull, one of the most prestigious battalion commanders in the division. In the centre of the same row, wearing his San Fernando Cross is Lieutenant Colonel Goméz-Zamalloa, one of the heroes of the Civil War. (FDA)

1940s and 1950s dealing with the treatment of frostbite was one written by a doctor who had served with the Blue Division. The percentage of Spanish losses resulting from frostbite or other conditions associated with extreme cold weather was high.

The fact that the Blue Division, composed as it was of men originating from a Mediterranean country, did not crumble in those terrible winter conditions is a tribute to its fighting spirit. In the second winter of 1943 the situation improved, as the Wehrmacht distributed adequate clothing and the division's new deployment (around Leningrad) near the Baltic Sea meant temperatures were not as low as those experienced the previous winter.

Veterans remembered the cold as one of the most difficult experiences of the campaign and it was always a matter of pride for them that they had overcome it.

Trench warfare

The Blue Division never participated in a blitzkrieg-type campaign and was destined to become involved in the desperate trench fighting undertaken by Army Group North from December 1941. Although the Spanish had not experienced the terrible trench war of World War I, this type of warfare had been common during the Civil War. However, in that conflict most of the areas covered by trenches had remained relatively quiet. Enemy trench raids had been infrequent and artillery duels of low intensity. Trench life had been simply tedious and uncomfortable, but generally low risk.

This was not to be the case on the Eastern Front. Although the great battles in the theatre were being fought in other sectors, fighting was continuous along the entire front. Raids conducted by units of company or even battalion strength were the order of the day and artillery support was often used. The titanic struggle between the Red Army and the Wehrmacht was being played out along every mile of front. Therefore, although maps appear to show the Blue Division to have been deployed in a sector that had become relatively stable as the months passed, it does not signify that the area was calm. Monthly casualty figures show that in most of those months in which the Blue Division was not involved in a major operation, the total of dead and wounded still reached the equivalent of a battalion.

Trench warfare also required great effort in constructing and maintaining the trenches in which the men were to live and fight. Veterans of the Blue Division remembered that such tasks were greatly disliked. The men had enlisted with the desire of being involved in a great adventure and handling picks and shovels was far from their expectations. In the frontline, they preferred to seek accommodation in the peasant dwellings found dotted around the area than dig bunkers. This was to cause casualties, as these wooden constructions were a favourite target for enemy artillery and they collapsed and burned with ease. The Germans observed the lack of interest amongst the Spanish for maintaining and improving

A group of volunteers poses near the Eiffel Tower on their journey home. They proudly display German decorations and insignia on their Spanish uniforms. (FDA)

PARIS 31 V 1942

their trenches. This attitude had been common in the Spanish Civil War in which the men on both sides had often expressed the sentiment that 'Spanish soldiers die on their feet, not hiding underground like rats', as an argument to justify their aversion to digging trenches.

The relief battalions: 1942–43

Like any combat unit, the Blue Division began receiving small contingents of reinforcements from almost the beginning of its existence, when, while the unit was still in Grafenwöhr, it became necessary to cover the personnel who had been rejected for service at the front. The terrible losses of early 1942 required the sending of significant numbers of replacements (three battalions) during the first three months of 1942.

In April 1942, the Spanish Army Minister, General Varela, for political motives that have already been mentioned, tried to organise a 'Second Division' to relieve the 'First Division' en masse. To this end, he ordered the recruitment and organisation of a large number of new battalions of volunteers who in the space of a few months were to relieve all the battalions of the original Blue Division. Neither General Muñoz Grandes nor the Germans approved of the idea. It seemed absurd to return soldiers who had become battle-hardened when it was expected that the Germans would return to the offensive when summer arrived on the Eastern Front. As soon as the march battalions reached the Eastern Front, they were disbanded and their effectives distributed among the division's different units. Therefore, the relief en masse of the division never occurred. From then on, instead of sending a large number of march battalions at the same time, their departure was staggered at regular intervals for Germany and the Eastern Front.

As happens in all the world's armies, the veterans (known as 'guripas', a word that means 'soldier' in Spanish military slang) received the new replacements with an air of superiority, calling them 'mortadelas'. The different sociological and psychological profile of the initial contingent (most of whom were students) and that of the march battalions (which were composed more and more of professional soldiers and peasants) emphasised the contrast between the two. It was feared that the new volunteers would not live up to the standard set by their predecessors. However, this was not to be the case. When the Blue Division fought the hardest engagement in its history at Krasny Bor, it was by then mainly composed of the so-called 'mortadelas', but still managed to pass the test.

In 1942, 19 march battalions arrived in Russia with 16,500 new volunteers and another eight battalions arrived in 1943 with a further 7,500 men. This enabled the Blue Division to maintain its strength at a level envied by

ON THE MOVE IN THE VOLKHOV POCKET

The campaign in Russia meant that the Spanish were confronted with terrain and climatic conditions previously unknown to them. The extremely cold winter of 1941–42 was a hard experience for the men of the Blue Division, coming as they did from a very different environment. Even with the arrival of the spring and summer of 1942 they had to operate in an environment that was equally inhospitable: the swampy forests around Volkhov. The Germans had named the area the 'Arsch der Welt'. There can be no doubt that during the course of the 20th century, the volunteers of the Blue Division fought in the most extreme environmental and climatic conditions experienced by Spanish troops. For veterans of the division, the very fact of surviving the experience was a source of great pride. While the fighting along the banks of the Volkhov and around Leningrad has never achieved the fame of Stalingrad or Kursk, this certainly does not imply that it was a quiet sector of the Eastern Front.

A gathering of veterans in Spain in 1943. They wear the belt and eagle of the Heer with their Falange uniforms, as well as the Blue Division shield and decorations won in Russia. (FDA)

neighbouring German divisions, which had had to modify their organisation from nine to six infantry battalions, whereas the Blue Division kept its original organisation of nine infantry battalions. Added to these was an additional unit, the reserve battalion ('Feldersatz Btl.', in German terminology), which the Spanish did not use as a depot unit, but rather as a shock force. Together with the II./269, the 250th Reserve Battalion was, without doubt, the most battle-hardened unit in the Blue Division.

The arrival of so many replacements not only permitted losses to be covered, but also allowed many veterans to be returned to Spain. Although volunteers had initially signed up for 'the duration of the campaign', the severity of the fighting in Russia made it advisable to introduce a system of rotation. At first, certain categories of men were returned to Spain (those least apt for continued service due to their physical condition, and those who had lost brothers, or were married men, etc.). Later, this was extended to all men who had completed a year's service. Eight battalions were repatriated during 1942, with another five returning up to October 1943.

By April 1943, all the men of the first contingent had been returned to Spain, with the exception of those who had expressed a desire to continue serving in the campaign. It was also common for many veterans to sign up and return to the front after arriving back in Spain.

As well as these march battalions, other much smaller groups of officers and NCOs were frequently sent between Spain and the Eastern Front to cover losses, as the need to replace these men was too urgent to wait for the arrival of a march battalion.

The system of rotation had positive effects as the establishments of the units were kept up to strength. Nevertheless, there were also problems: there was a constant need to train the new arrivals in the realities of the front and, as has occurred in all armies who have employed this system of rotation, those soldiers with only a short time left to complete their tour of duty became risk averse and lost their aggressiveness.

The repatriation of veterans caused a particular problem in the case of officers, as rotation among them was more frequent than with the rank and file. The idea was that the campaign in Russia would serve to train the greatest number of officers possible in modern tactics and weapons. It was not uncommon, for example, that the same company had three or four different captains in the period of a year. These captains were, in some cases, replaced due to death or injury, and in others because of rotation.

Muñoz Grandes with one of his officers. Adored by the ordinary soldiers of the division, his officers feared his temper; he would not hesitate to reprimand them publicly if he felt they were not paying sufficient attention to the conditions of their men. (FDA)

When the order was given for the division to return to Spain and to be substituted by the Blue Legion, the volunteers for the Legion were told that there would be no more reliefs. It was stated that the unit would stay at the front until 'its extinction in combat'. Such a gloomy prospect significantly affected the morale of its men.

Support services

When the Blue Division left for the front, it left an 'Ersatzkommando' established in the city of Hof to look after the personal effects of its men (their uniforms) and to take charge of bureaucratic tasks involved with wounded and sick men returning to Spain.

Later, when the march battalions began arriving with new volunteers, and with the start of the large-scale return of men in the repatriation battalions, this 'Erstazkommando' at Hof became more and more important until it was converted into a depot battalion. It was in Hof that the newly arrived volunteers received their weapons, uniforms and documentation. Those

The second commander-in-chief of the Blue Division was General Esteban-Infantes, a man with a distinctly different personality to Muñoz Grandes. Here he is seen presenting a Spanish decoration to Field Marshal Georg von Küchler, Commander of Army Group North. (FDA)

returning home handed in all their German-issued equipment and uniforms and recovered their Spanish uniforms.

As the campaign went on, it became more frequent for Spanish soldiers to find themselves in the rear (as sick or wounded, on leave, in transit, etc.). In order to attend to them, and given the language barrier (very few understood German), the Blue Division established a series of 'Representaciones' (delegations). These were offices that took responsibility for attending to the needs of Spanish soldiers (food, accommodation, etc.) in different cities in the Baltic States (Tallinn in Estonia, Riga in Latvia, and Vilna in Lithuania) and Germany (Berlin, Königsberg and Hof).

Finally, in the summer of 1942, the staff of the Blue Division created a Rearguard Services Command, which coordinated the tasks of the depot battalion in Hof, the delegations and also the Spanish hospitals and military police detachments in the rear area.

Medical services

The Blue Division left Spain with a medical group made up of two medical companies. When they arrived in Grafenwöhr, they found that each German medical group also had its own field hospital ('Feldlazarett'), something that in Spain only existed at the Army corps level. Staff for its organisation were dispatched urgently from Spain, joining the division before its departure for Russia. The Blue Division's doctors were very impressed with the technical resources at the disposal of the Wehrmacht's medical groups.

As soon as the Blue Division arrived at the front and began military operations, the Spanish started to suffer a high rate of losses, certainly a larger number than had been expected. Evacuation to the rear was by German hospital trains and the Spanish soldiers were cared for in German 'Kriegslazarette' (evacuation or war hospitals) with the obvious language problems this entailed. Already in October 1941, a Spanish evacuation hospital had been set up in Porkhov (east of Pskov). Simultaneously, a small Spanish 'Reservelazarett' (general or convalescent hospital) was being organised in Berlin, with Spanish military doctors and nurses assigned to both. Nevertheless, neither the Porkhov Hospital nor the one in Berlin were enough to deal with the high number of casualties. Therefore, a large number of wounded, sick or frostbitten men had to go to German military hospitals in Russia, the Baltic countries or Germany. Despite language difficulties, the Spaniards were satisfied with the treatment they received from the Germans in the different 'Kriegslazarette' or 'Reservelazarette' in which they were cared for.

 THE BATTLE OF KRASNY BOR (10 FEBRUARY 1943)

At Krasny Bor the Spanish suffered an onslaught from the Red Army they had never before experienced. The artillery bombardment was especially heavy, and they were considerably outnumbered by the mass of infantry unleashed against them. However, it was the Soviet tanks (T-34s and KV-1s) that finally broke through their lines. Almost all the Blue Division's anti-tank guns were 37mm pieces, plus some captured examples of larger calibre. All were inadequate for the task of stopping the Soviet armour.

A Spanish engineer corporal, Antonio Ponte Anido (in the centre foreground), was awarded the San Fernando Cross for his part in taking on these steel monsters. On observing a Russian tank about to attack a first-aid post housing many defenceless wounded men, he raced to place anti-tank mines under its tracks. The ensuing explosion stopped the tank, but also resulted in his death.

Although the Spanish troops were impressed by the quality of the arms with which the Germans equipped the Blue Division, they soon came to appreciate that Soviet weapons were often more reliable and hard-wearing. The PPSh submachine gun (carried by the bottom left figure) and the Degtaryev DP light machine gun (carried by the standing soldier) were especially appreciated.

The German general Kleffel, commander of L Army Corps, speaking in the welcome address given to a Spanish march battalion that has just arrived at the front. General Esteban-Infantes, in contrast to Muñoz Grandes, was always perfectly uniformed. (FDA)

From January 1942, a network of Spanish military hospitals was created in the rear area and staffed by Spanish doctors and nurses. These hospitals were to provide 2,000 beds. The Porkhov Spanish 'Kriegslazarett' was closed and new Spanish hospitals were created in cities more to the rear, in Riga and Vilna. The small Berlin Spanish 'Reservelazarett' remained operational, but a much bigger one was set up in Königsberg (East Prussia), and a new convalescent hospital was established in Hof, where the Blue Division 'Ersatzkommando' was located.

When the Blue Division was deployed near Leningrad, Spanish medical staff were posted to the two German 'Kriegslazarette' nearest to its sector, in order to attend to the hospitalised troops waiting to be sent to a facility further behind the front (Riga, Vilna or Königsberg). An Inspectorate of Spanish Military Hospitals, with its headquarters in Berlin, coordinated work in all the Spanish hospitals.

A certain number of wounded and maimed, those with particularly difficult problems, continued to be attended to in specialized German military hospitals, even after the repatriation of the Blue Division.

In the Königsberg and Hof hospitals, there were mixed Spanish–German medical boards to determine which individuals had to be discharged because of medical reasons. In the case that they were discharged, they went back to Spain to be attended to in military hospitals or to return home.

For the Spanish volunteers, it was comforting to learn of the good treatment that their wounded received from the German medical services. There was a habit in Spain of sending men back to their units as soon as they started to recover. However, in German hospitals, the sick and wounded soldiers were cared for until they had made a full recovery, in order to avoid any problems once they had returned to their units. The Spanish finally adopted the same policy as the Germans about their casualties. In addition, logically, Spanish volunteers preferred to be attended to in their own hospitals, where they could live together with their comrades, be looked after by Spanish staff and receive food prepared to their own tastes.

There was also a pleasant surprise for the hospitalised Spaniards, in the form of the great support they received from the civilian population in Germany. They received visits from boys and girls from the Hitlerjugend at the hospitals, theatre or cabaret plays were organized for them and, when they had better recovered, they were able to go on excursions or were invited by German families to spend a few days with them.

Of the almost 5,000 deaths in the Blue Division, about 1,500 died in their own field hospitals or in the other Spanish hospitals from the seriousness of their wounds. Between August 1941 and October 1943, the non-mortal Spanish losses were approximately 9,500 wounded, 8,400 sick and injured, and 1,500 suffering from frostbite. Among these, more than 2,000 were crippled to varying degrees of severity. The Spanish volunteers who were severely maimed (for example, losing both legs) received orthopaedic prostheses in specialised German clinics.

Between October 1941 and February 1942, and due to the unexpectedly high number of losses resulting from the hard fighting and frostbite, as well as the total collapse of the German logistic infrastructure in Russia because of the prolonged campaign, there was a certain level of disorganisation in the evacuation of Spanish casualties. Nevertheless, from February 1942 onwards the Blue Division's medical services worked correctly. In summary, thousands of Spanish volunteers were able to receive adequate attention thanks to the Spanish and German medical services, which made it easier to endure the dramatic experiences they were going through.

Discipline

Just like any division in the Heer, the Blue Division had a detachment of military police. This detachment was composed of members of the 'Guardia Civil' (Civil Guard), a Spanish Security Corps organised along military lines (similar to the French Gendarmerie or the Italian Carabinieri). The 'Guardia Civil' enjoyed a high reputation in Spain; it was attached as military police to the Blue Division and operated in the area in which the division was deployed.

When the Blue Division was created, an agreement was reached with the Germans that would allow the Spanish military justice code to be applied instead of that of the Germans. Spanish volunteers could only be detained by the Spanish Military Police and tried under Spanish military law.

A group of convalescing Blue Division soldiers visits a factory in Germany. Great efforts were made to present positive aspects of the Third Reich to the Spanish. (FDA)

A group of volunteers read *Marca*, a Spanish sport daily that regularly reached the frontline. A large number of Spanish newspapers were sent to Russia to maintain the troops' morale. (FDA)

When Spanish troops began to appear in large numbers in the rear area (hospitalised men and soldiers in transit between Spain and Russia), this started to create problems. In the eyes of the Germans, the Spanish were undisciplined; they failed to salute German officers, were rowdy in bars, left the hospitals without permission to visit the cities, and wore their uniforms in a manner against regulations. The rigid German discipline was alien to the Spanish volunteers.

Therefore, it was decided to create new detachments of Spanish Military Police in those towns and cities where there was a significant Spanish presence (Riga, Vilna, Königsberg and Hof). They were also stationed along the route from Spain to the Eastern Front, starting at Hendaye (on the Franco-Spanish border), via Paris and Berlin to a series of locations in Russia and the Baltic States. These small detachments were also formed by men of the Civil Guard, who were well respected by the volunteers due to the prestige of this corps in Spain. Thanks to the work of these detachments, the movement of thousands of volunteers from the Franco-Spanish border to the Russian Front was well ordered. However, some Spanish volunteers took advantage of the free rail travel for soldiers and the good will of the Germans towards the Spanish shield worn on their uniform to travel part way around Europe before the Spanish Military Police could detain them.

MOTIVATION AND MORALE

Although the Blue Division was a volunteer unit with strong anti-communist convictions, this did not mean that their level of fighting spirit maintained itself automatically. The tough conditions at the front could certainly affect the men's morale. However, the main problem experienced in the division was a feeling of homesickness and being surrounded by people they could not understand (Germans, Russians and the inhabitants of the Baltic States). Although leave back to Spain was granted, it was infrequent given the number of men who served in Russia. Apart from this, when the campaign in Russia began to turn against the Axis, it became necessary to combat the effect this had on the volunteers. In order to maintain morale, several measures were taken.

Food

Spanish cuisine is completely unlike that of both Germany and Russia, and the Spanish are devoted to their gastronomy. Problems began to emerge when the volunteers arrived in Grafenwöhr. The men found the typical German diet detestable and to minimise this problem food, drink and tobacco were sent from Spain so that the volunteers at least received some products that were to their taste.

Although the arrival of this food and other Spanish products was often random, as the transport depended on the German logistics network,

One of the division's medical officers giving instructions to Spanish nurses. The Blue Division had its own hospitals in Germany and the Baltic countries. (FDA)

Presents being distributed to patients in the Blue Division's Berlin 'Reservelazarett'. (FDA)

Volunteers in Russia performing a pantomime of the most famous of Spanish spectacles, the bullfight. (FDA)

something arrived most months. These products were added to the supplies of the German Quartermaster Corps, which corresponded to a unit of this type. The Spanish volunteers, like all soldiers on campaign, often complained of being hungry, but in reality, the diet they received in Russia was quite good.

The Christmas celebration in Spain is accompanied by the consumption of sweets and special liqueurs. So that this would be available to the troops, a special 'Christmas box' was sent from Spain with all the typical seasonal extras. Due to the logistic chaos reigning in Russia, the 1941 'Christmas box' was not distributed to the men until February 1942. This did not re-occur at Christmas 1942. The distribution of these festive parcels had a great psychological effect on the men who were so far from their homes and families at such a special time of year.

Religious services

For right-wing Spaniards, Catholicism is more than just religion: it forms part of the national identity. The terrible persecution of the Catholic Church by the Popular Front before and during the Civil War had simply strengthened the religious feeling of those who supported the Nationalist cause during the conflict, which was treated as a crusade against the 'Godless'. The Blue Division was imbued with that same crusading spirit against Marxist atheism. This was another shared feature of those who made up the Blue Division, whether they happened to be members of the Falange, professional army officers, simple country peasants or from the elite Spanish Legion.

The aspect of the Blue Division's organisation that most differed from that of a German division was in the number of military chaplains. A German division only had one protestant and one catholic chaplain for the entire division. The Blue Division had one chaplain for each battalion or group. A chaplain was also assigned to each Spanish hospital deployed in the rear.

All important acts were accompanied by a mass, with attendance being compulsory. Other masses held in the field, organised on Sundays and religious festivals, were voluntary, but were always well attended. The Catholic religious calendar was celebrated with devotion in Russia and it did not lack processions, in which officers and men would parade behind their chaplains as if they were back in Spain.

This deep religious feeling meant that the Spanish sympathised greatly with the Poles and Lithuanians, when they marched through these countries on the way to the front. For the Spanish, it seemed incomprehensible that the Germans had not been able to encourage the Poles, as catholic and anti-communist as they were, to participate in the anti-communist crusade. The Spanish were also surprised to find that many of the Russians they encountered had kept their religious beliefs intact, despite Soviet propaganda. Icons, those typical Byzantine-inspired paintings found in great numbers in Russian houses, fascinated them. Many of these icons were bought by the Spanish volunteers and taken home, and for many veterans they were to become the most emotive souvenirs of the campaign in Russia.

Spanish and German propaganda
The Spanish volunteers of the Blue Division were greatly impressed by the Heer's propaganda machine, equipped as it was with resources that were unimaginable in Spain. The Blue Division had hardly reached the frontline when General Muñoz Grandes gave the order for the division to create its own weekly publication, the *Hoja de Campaña* (*Campaign Sheet*), for the Spanish volunteers in Russia. The publication had modest beginnings, being printed on a duplicator, but was later published by a printer in Riga, then in Tallinn. It continued to be published until the Blue Legion was disbanded.

Given the level of education of many members of the division, it was not

A returning battalion of veterans arrives in Irún. At centre is Colonel Pimentel, who had commanded the 262nd Regiment. The woman on the left is Celia Giménez, a popular commentator on Radio Berlin, who played an important role in the propaganda effort related to the Blue Division. The contingents of veterans who returned in 1942 and 1943 were given large public receptions. This was not to be the case in 1944. (FDA)

The 25th March Battalion arrives at the front. In 1943 the number of volunteers fell, but there were always volunteers ready to go to Russia. When the order to repatriate the Blue Division was given in October 1943, the 28th March Battalion had already been organized in Spain and was waiting to begin their journey to the front – but it would never leave. (FDA)

difficult to find some excellent writers. Its exceptional presentation and the quality of the writing soon converted *Hoja de Campaña* into a reputable publication. Apart from the military/political articles on the development of the war, there was also abundant information on Spain (including the results of the Spanish Football League) and the paper facilitated the possibility of establishing contact with young Spanish women who wanted to become 'war godmothers'. *Hoja de Campaña* was, therefore, decisive in combating homesickness amongst the ranks of the volunteers. Many copies were sent back to Spain, as it provided magnificent propaganda for the Blue Division.

The Blue Division's library was also administered through the publication, which meant volunteers could read books in their own language, which alleviated the boredom in the trenches. However, like soldiers the world over, what the volunteers liked to do most to relieve the boredom was playing cards or reading and writing letters home.

A Spanish officer observes the enemy lines. The constant rotation of officers, which was a policy to give as many of them as possible experience in modern warfare, was to have a detrimental effect on the unit. (FDA)

The German military propaganda machine made great efforts on behalf of the Spanish. They provided all the means necessary to produce *Hoja de Campaña* and there was a detachment of 'Kriegsberichter' in the German Liaison Staff, which incidentally formed the only German unit assigned to the Blue Division. Richly illustrated pamphlets were produced on the Spanish volunteer, some of which were printed in both Spanish and German, together with postcard collections and other propaganda items that were distributed among the volunteers with the objective of boosting their morale.

Furthermore, the Blue Division was a boon for German propaganda as it enabled them to portray the campaign in Russia as an anti-communist crusade, as the Spanish volunteers had come from a neutral country. The Blue Division became a commonly referred to theme in the German military magazine *Signal* (especially the Spanish edition, of which thousands of copies were distributed among the men of the division, and many thousands more back in Spain itself).

Great efforts were made to extol the Spanish volunteers in Russia as Allied propaganda, especially the BBC's Spanish broadcasts, launched constant campaigns to discredit the Blue Division or ran alarmist news stories (on several occasions the division was reported as having been annihilated). To counter this, the Deutscher Rundfunk made daily reports in its Spanish service about the Blue Division. Through these broadcasts the volunteers could even transmit messages (previously recorded by the 'Kriegsberichter') for their families. There were Spanish radio stations that joined in with this exchange of messages, broadcasting programmes that could be received in the trenches in Russia so that families in Spain could send greetings and news to the volunteers.

Mail

The highly efficient German Feldpost (field post) was another source of joy to the Spanish volunteers. Without any doubt, the Spanish received more mail than any of the neighbouring German units. Not only families, but also the many 'war godmothers' (almost every volunteer had several of them) sent thousands of cards each month. The men received local newspapers from every province and major city in Spain. As they belonged to the only Spanish Division present on the Eastern Front the whole country was focused on them, and so the volunteers received not just letters and newspapers, but also a large number of parcels containing food and clothes.

Awards and decorations

One of the most common methods of raising morale is the award of decorations. As a unit of the Spanish Army, the Blue Division had the right to be awarded Spanish decorations; and as a volunteer force integrated in the Wehrmacht its men were also entitled to German awards. Spanish decorations awarded to volunteers were, in order of importance, the San Fernando Cross and the Military Medal (given as both individual awards and for unit citations), the War Cross with Palm Leaves, the War Cross and the Red Cross for Military Merit. In the two first cases, these awards required a long process to be followed before their concession, sometimes taking years. The San Fernando

Spanish assault engineers undergoing training. The constant arrival of new volunteers made it necessary to keep up a continuous training programme. (FDA)

A group of Spanish volunteers in the trenches around Leningrad. Their disinterest in complying with the regulations regarding uniform is apparent. Many display the 'yoke and arrows', while one is carrying a Soviet submachine gun. The Spanish greatly appreciated these resilient Russian weapons. (FDA)

Cross was finally awarded to eight members of the Blue Division, seven of whom had been killed in action. This figure may appear small, but it should be compared with the number of these awards conceded by the Nationalist Army during the Civil War, which totalled 71, among an army in which 1,200,000 men served. 42 individual Military Medals and two collective Military Medals were also awarded to the Blue Division. Many other recommendations for the San Fernando Cross and Military Medal were rejected because from 1943 the war clearly began to go against Germany, and Franco's regime decided it would be expedient to desist from extolling the Blue Division in order to avoid provoking the Allies.

However, the members of the Blue Division showed a special interest in obtaining German awards, especially the much-admired Iron Cross. According to German records, the members of the Blue Division were awarded 2,370 examples of the Iron Cross 2nd Class and 138 of the Iron Cross 1st Class. However, the documentation is incomplete. With documents available in Spain, it is possible to reach figures that are more realistic – about 2,500 and 150 respectively. The War Merit Cross with Swords (both 2nd and 1st Class), were awarded to Spanish volunteers in similar numbers.

If the division had not been awarded Spanish decorations, the figures would have been even higher. However, normal practice for the Blue Division high command was not to request Wehrmacht decorations for its men until they had received Spanish awards. Apart from the Iron Cross, another much-appreciated German decoration was the 'Infanterie Sturmabzeichen'.

In 1943, the Oberkommando der Wehrmacht had a commemorative medal struck for the Spanish Volunteers, which in itself was exceptional, given that no other unit of foreign volunteers was given similar consideration on the part of the German high command. That same year, the Spanish government ordered a campaign medal for Russia. All veterans who completed their service honourably were to receive both awards. Another decoration widely bestowed on the Spanish volunteers was the Order of the German Eagle, specifically created by the German government to be bestowed on foreign citizens. In fact, many members of the Blue Division already had been given the decoration prior to the campaign in Russia, as it had been awarded during the Spanish Civil War.

ON CAMPAIGN

Relations with German soldiers

At an official level and in propaganda, the Germans had always been complimentary towards the Blue Division. Hitler had even praised the division in some of his speeches. However, this was not the case in confidential German documents. Several of the officers of the German Liaison Staff formed very critical opinions, especially in regard to the capabilities of Spanish officers and

General Esteban-Infantes (with field service cap), together with the chief of the German Liaison Staff, Colonel Knüppel (with 'Schirmmütze'). They are accompanied by Spanish and German officers. (FDA)

the discipline of the men. The same occurred with some commanders of the army corps in which the Blue Division was integrated. The reports are almost identical to those issued by German officers serving with the armies of Romania, Italy and Hungary operating on the Eastern Front, or with the volunteer legions of European anti-communists forming part of the Heer or Waffen-SS. It is worth bearing in mind that these German officers were expressing the real, or imagined, deficiencies of these military forces from the point of view of men who perceived themselves to be members of the best army in the world.

The Germans were particularly preoccupied with the perceived lack of discipline of Spanish troops in the rear areas. The Prussian traditions of discipline seemed very alien to the Spanish, so it is not surprising that the Germans saw things the way they did. However, there is another aspect that cannot be ignored – the racist views that predominated in Germany at that time. In the eyes of many Germans, the Spanish volunteers, olive-skinned and short in stature as they were, appeared like gypsies who were far too undignified to be wearing German uniforms. Worse, they 'dishonoured' their uniforms because they wore them with no respect for regulations.

The accusation that discipline in the Blue Division was relaxed was based partly in truth. Spanish commanders did not find it easy to punish men who had volunteered and travelled halfway across Europe in order to fight communism for what appeared to be minor infractions. A good example is the case of an NCO, a master armourer in a Spanish battalion. During the winter of 1942, finding that the MG34s were not functioning correctly, the man decided to make his own alterations to the weapons, cutting off part of the recoil spring. When the Germans of the Liaison Staff inspected the battalion's weapons, which was a regular practice, they accused the NCO of sabotaging the armament and demanded

One of the Blue Division's most famous personalities, Captain Urbano Gómez García, displaying his many German decorations. He wears the emblem of his parent unit, the Spanish Foreign Legion, above his left breast pocket. (FDA)

that he be punished accordingly. Far from complying with the request, the Spanish decorated him for showing the initiative to make sure the weapons worked effectively.

Nevertheless, the commanders of the Blue Division were only too well aware that Germany was judging Spain on the actions of their men and so they took energetic measures. Hundreds of volunteers were returned to Spain classified as 'undesirables'. The grounds for being classed as such were varied: suspicion of holding left-wing sympathies, venereal disease, resistance to discipline and homosexuality, amongst others. Minor infractions were dealt with at the front, in a company tasked with the loading and unloading of supplies. Serious offences meant prison, the sentence to be served in a Spanish military prison (as was the case with 100 men of the Blue Division). Some very serious offences, such as desertion and self-wounding, were punished with the death penalty, which was applied in only a few cases.

Relations between German and Spanish military personnel in the rear areas could become stormy at times. The fights in the bars of Königsberg, between Spanish troops recovering from wounds and U-boat crews who were trained in the Baltic Sea, became famous. These fights almost always revolved around the pursuit of women.

When the Spanish arrived in Grafenwöhr they were exceedingly well disposed towards the Germans. However, complaints were not long in coming. The fact of being equipped as a horse-drawn division and marching to the front on foot seemed a sign of contempt, although in reality most of the Heer operated in exactly the same way. The simple act of being equipped with ankle boots and gaiters instead of the famous jackboots was perceived as an injustice, even though all the German units being organised at that time were being issued the same footwear.

Once at the Front, Spanish soldiers occasionally expressed the sentiment that they were being used as cannon fodder, which was false, as for Germany the political disadvantages that would result from the destruction of the Spanish Division outweighed any advantages that could be obtained from using the volunteers in this fashion.

What in fact upset the Spanish volunteers most was the hard, often criminal, treatment meted out by the Germans to the Poles, Jews and Russians. The German order that became the most disobeyed by the Spanish volunteers was undoubtedly that of non-fraternisation with the Jewish population.

DAILY LIFE IN RUSSIA
All the veterans of the Blue Division were in agreement that they marched to Russia to defeat communism and not to fight the Russian people. Although relations between a foreign army of occupation and the population of that occupied nation can never be ideal, the relationship between the Spanish troops and Russian civilians was notably cordial. In the areas in which they were deployed, the Spanish troops lived alongside the elderly, women and children, whose difficult situation moved the Spanish volunteers. The volunteers did not as a rule hold any prejudice against Slavs in general and the Russians in particular, given that Spain had never been in conflict with them. As the Spanish preferred to live in the peasant cabins ('isbas') rather than dig bunkers, relations between them and the families with whom they were billeted became close, and the volunteers shared food with them. This behaviour, coupled with the scarce interest displayed by the Spanish in following German regulations regarding uniform, profoundly irritated the Germans.

The two NCOs in the left of this illustration are wearing the collars of their shirts over their field grey tunics. One of them, a Falangist, is wearing his blue shirt; the other, a veteran of the Spanish Foreign Legion, the green shirt of his parent unit. Nostalgia for home is clearly demonstrated by the poster advertising a bullfight in the upper left.

Major Miguel Román Garrido was one of the heroes of the Blue Division. He was an officer in the 'Regulares'. He won many German decorations for his actions in Russia, as well as the Spanish Individual Military Medal. His battalion, the II./269, was awarded the Collective Military Medal. (FDA)

As wounded soldiers began returning home during the autumn of 1941, they described the terrible reality of what was occurring in the occupied countries of Eastern Europe to the Spanish authorities. All the books written by veterans of the Blue Division contain a condemnation of German conduct in this regard. However, the men of the Blue Division were only partially aware of what was going on; their movement through the occupied zones was rapid. The only towns and cities in the rear areas where the volunteers could spend any period of time were the capitals of the Baltic States, and the German occupation of Estonia, Latvia and Lithuania was far less repressive than in any of the regions of the Soviet Union.

The Spanish volunteers did not come to know the true dimensions of the problem and thought that the bitter struggle against communism lay behind Germany's policies.

Therefore, in spite of this, they still held the Wehrmacht in high esteem. As fervent anti-communists, they could not forget the fact that while they held a small sector of the front, it was the Germans who were bearing the brunt of the fighting against the Red Army along thousands of kilometres of frontline. Far more than those remaining behind in Spain, the members of the Blue Division were fully aware of the titanic effort being made by the Wehrmacht on the Eastern Front. Although the Wehrmacht, seen from the inside, was not the formidable armoured war machine portrayed by German propaganda, the Spanish volunteers admired its efficiency. When, at the end of 1943, the division began the process of repatriation, the reality of the situation in their eyes was the fact that the Red Army continued to be encircled and contained within Leningrad. Few could imagine that in less than a year and a half the Red Army would occupy Berlin.

Relations with Russia's civilian population

When reading many of the numerous books written by veterans of the Blue Division, one of the most striking aspects is the great affection with which they describe the Russian people. Soon after arriving in Russia, the Spanish troops quickly learned to distinguish between what for them was the hateful, communist regime and the Russian people.

However, it cannot be forgotten that they formed part of an occupying army. Some Spanish troops did commit excesses against civilians, searching for food, cold-weather clothing or sexual satisfaction, but this was never common practice and such cases were few in number.

It was not the case that the Spanish soldiers were in any way morally superior to their German comrades. If the Blue Division had been fighting in North Africa, the reality would have been very different, given that the majority of Spaniards held strong racial prejudice against the inhabitants of North Africa. However, Spain had never been involved in a prior conflict with Russia and the Spanish were devoid of any prejudice towards the Slavs in general or Russians in particular.

When the Red Army attacked the Blue Division at Krasny Bor, the few inhabitants who had remained in the locality helped them as much as they could. This was not strange; since their arrival in the sector, Spanish commanders had given their orders to the battalion kitchens deployed there (those of the 262nd Regiment) to reserve part of the daily rations for the children and elderly (who had died by the thousands the previous winter) in the area. The Soviet Union never made any accusations of war crimes or crimes against humanity to which the Blue Division could be held responsible.

Therefore, it should not be considered strange that in 2005, to commemorate the end of World War II, a delegation of veterans of the Blue Division was officially invited to attend the acts to mark the event in St Petersburg.

Prisoners and deserters

The Red Army captured 464 Spanish soldiers between 1941 and 1945 (the last of them in the battle for Berlin). Bearing in mind that more than 45,000 men served with the Blue Division, Blue Legion and the clandestine units that existed from 1944, it becomes clear that the Spanish obviously preferred death to capture. Of this total, approximately 70 were in actual fact deserters who wished to go over to the Soviets. Desertion, as can be seen, was a rare phenomenon in the Blue Division.

The harsh conditions on the Eastern Front and the intense propaganda campaign carried out against the Blue Division, in which advantages were offered to those who deserted, led to a handful of volunteers taking this step. These men committed the worst error of their lives, as the Soviets kept them in

One Spanish captain and two junior officers in the Blue Division trenches south of Leningrad. Contrary to regulations, none of them are wearing their helmets. Also, against German regulations, we notice their jackets are open at the collar. This was usual practice in order to show the Falange blue shirt (as per the captain in the centre of image) or the light green shirt from the Spanish Foreign Legion (as per the 2nd Lieutenant). (FDA)

55

A march battalion celebrating mass in Hof before leaving for the Russian front. The Spanish lived their Russian campaign as a 'holy crusade' against communism. It was Catholicism more than any political idea that unified the Spanish volunteers. (FDA)

captivity until 1954, the same date as the other prisoners. In a few cases, men were held until 1956. Long before this date, the Soviets had freed almost all of the prisoners pertaining to Germany's allies and members of other units of anti-communist volunteers recruited in Europe. Franco's regime never recognised the Soviet Union, a country with which Spain never established diplomatic relations. The USSR never granted these captives the rights of prisoners of war and, as a result, they never received letters from their families and in the majority of cases, they were officially reported as dead. The repatriation of those who had spent from 9 to 13 years in the Gulags did not happen until after Stalin's death.

Captivity in Russia was to prove a dreadful experience, which cost the lives of 130 Spanish prisoners. There were many protests made, which insisted on their recognition as prisoners of war. Being a very small minority in the Gulags, they could not count on much support from comrades, although they established very good relations with some of the Germans, and above all with the Italians.

The arrival in Spain of released prisoners was a major event, and thousands of people were waiting for them. One officer, Captain Palacios, published his memoirs of his time in captivity in a book titled *Ambassador in Hell*, which has gone through many editions in Spanish, been translated into several European languages and been adapted into a screenplay. The fight for survival of these men was to be the last battle of the Blue Division.

AFTERMATH

Repatriation

The first battalions to arrive back in Spain in 1942 were cause for a massive reception of the type that had seen them off in 1941. When the last battalions of the Blue Legion returned home in the spring of 1944, hardly anyone turned out to greet them. The war had clearly gone against the Germans and many suspected a change of regime would be inevitable in Spain; therefore, those men who had not so long ago been fêted as the heroes of a 'new Spain' were now viewed as a potential source of embarrassment.

When the Allies liberated France, the future of Franco's regime seemed bleak. The Spanish Government made all imaginable gestures in an attempt to improve relations with Britain and the United States. To evoke the memory of the Blue Division and its fallen became highly taboo after 1945. For example, the former Minister of Foreign Affairs, Serrano Suñer, who had been the main proponent of the Blue Division, published his memoirs of the World War II period without even mentioning the unit. Several ex-combatants reacted against this by publishing their books on the Russian campaign, stating their pride in having fought on the Eastern Front. For these men it was humiliating to be treated in this way. However, in reality they were lucky; anti-communist volunteers in other European countries who had joined the Heer or Waffen-SS often faced severe punishment.

The Spanish did not tend to wear decorations with their combat uniforms. However, the Blue Division decided to adopt this German custom. Apart from his awards, this NCO wears a small SEU badge on his breast pocket. Over his shoulder he carries an MG42, a weapon which greatly impressed the Spanish. (FDA)

A volunteer nails the regulation Blue Division shield on the grave-marker of a comrade. The shield he himself wears is non-regulation, as he has added the 'yoke and arrows' of the Falange and an Iron Cross. (FDA)

A member of the Blue Division's 'Feldgendarmie'. A sign behind him indicates the way to the 'Cuartel General' (general headquarters) of the DEV ('División Española de Voluntarios', Spanish Volunteer Division), the official name of the Blue Division. (FDA)

At the end of World War II, Spain was not admitted to the United Nations, and the USA, the United Kingdom and France withdrew their ambassadors from Madrid. However, the Cold War was on the horizon and the kind of fervent anti-communism typical of Franco's regime soon became acceptable.

While Spain never joined NATO, from 1953 it signed military treaties with the USA, and American bases were set up in the country. General Eisenhower, as president of the USA, and General De Gaulle, as president of France, both visited Spain and did not hesitate to embrace Franco.

The return of prisoners from Russia brought the Blue Division back to public attention, if only for a few months, in books, reports in the press, and even a few films. When, in 1956, Hungary rebelled against Soviet occupation, the government in Madrid thought the USA would lead a new anti-communist crusade and even offered to provide a new 'Blue Division'. However, it did not take long for Spanish leaders to understand that, for western governments, the Blue Division was an uncomfortable relic, given that it had fought under the banners of the Third Reich. Therefore, this episode of history was again pushed into the shadows.

The diffusion of information on the scale and horror of the crimes committed by the Third Reich placed the veterans of the Blue Division in an uncomfortable situation. Although they were in no way responsible for these crimes, there was no shortage of those who wished to present them as such for having worn the German uniform.

The defeat of the Axis made the possibility of realising the Falangist revolution evaporate completely. The ambitions of recovering Gibraltar or the dream of extending Spain's possessions in Africa were dashed. Many former volunteers felt as though they had been deceived by the promises that had been made when the Blue Division was created. The most ardent Falangists criticised Franco for not trying to extend a policy of social justice or carrying out the complete modernisation of Spain. Some even went as far as to completely break with Franco and the Falange and join the ranks of the opposition. However, with the Red Army camped on the Elbe and China also having a communist regime, the majority of Blue Division veterans considered the threat of communism to be greater than ever, and opted to remain loyal to Franco's regime. Many of them occupied positions of political responsibility or important military posts. They resigned themselves to accepting the order to remove all Wehrmacht insignia from their uniforms, which many had continued to wear since their repatriation in 1942 and 1944. Nevertheless, they continued to display the decorations they had won in Russia and the Blue Division shield, which became a symbol of great pride.

Veteran associations

From 1954, veterans of the Blue Division began to form associations all over Spain. They held meetings, opened veterans' clubs and published bulletins. Thousands of veterans joined these associations, but a few years later they began to reduce their activities. Franco's regime had no interest in making the episode an important part of its history, so these associations were allowed to languish. However, during their existence they had been the most active veteran organisations in Spain, far more so than those associations of Nationalist Army veterans from the Civil War. The intensity of their experience in Russia no doubt explains this fact. Many veterans of the Blue Division had taken part in the Civil War (especially officers and NCOs) and they had always emphasised that even the hardest fighting in the Civil War paled in comparison with that on the Eastern Front.

Only a handful of men regretted their past, stating to journalists that they had enlisted out of hunger or to help family members who had become victims of Franco's regime. Had Germany won World War II, such declarations would probably have been very different.

For Spaniards, the story of the Blue Division is in many ways the final act of the Civil War. Those who sympathise with the Popular Front do everything possible to denigrate the Division, while those who seek to justify the Nationalist Uprising of 18 July 1936 attempt to ennoble it. Both of these views are minority ones. The majority of Spaniards simply concede the volunteers of the Blue Division respect for being willing to sacrifice themselves for their ideals, irrespective of whether they share these ideals or not.

The fall of communism in Russia and Eastern Europe from 1991 onwards filled former volunteers with pride;

Colonel Antonio García Navarro was the division's last chief of staff and later went on to command the Blue Legion. Like many other officers, he wore the Spanish rather than the German belt. (FDA)

history appeared to have shown them to be right. Soon after, the veterans' associations created a Blue Division foundation that achieved two long-sought goals. A monument to the fallen was erected in a cemetery in Madrid, which provides the last resting place of an unknown volunteer whose remains were brought back from Russia. Franco's regime had never done anything similar to this. In Russia, a Spanish military cemetery was established near Novgorod, which now holds the remains of many Blue Division soldiers. The cemetery has become a place of pilgrimage for veterans and the families of the fallen.

At the time of writing of this book, a curious phenomenon has arisen in Spain. When the division's few remaining survivors pass away, on the wishes of the deceased, when the obituary is published in the press, there is no mention of their career, qualifications or honours, only the simple phrase: 'Veteran of the Blue Division'.

The written legacy

Thousands of volunteers had received a university education when they left for Russia, and thousands more resumed their studies when they returned. Conscious of the fact that the experience of the Eastern Front was sure to be one of the most important in their lives, many kept detailed campaign diaries. With their education and the raw material of their diaries, many went on to write books. Several dozens have been published to date through one means or another: from modest private editions to genuine best-sellers printed by major Spanish publishers, including those appearing as instalments in magazines and bulletins. What is no less surprising is that new books keep appearing. Now it is the children and grandchildren of volunteers who edit writings long forgotten in a desk drawer. Other material has never even achieved the form of a manuscript, and has been lost among family archives or has only been made available to a handful of investigators. Without doubt, no other Spanish military unit has originated such a flow of literature. Thanks to this, the experiences of the Blue Division soldiers are easily accessible, provided, of course, that the reader is able to understand Spanish.

VETERANS

The extreme harshness of the campaign in Russia inevitably led to a strong sense of comradeship amongst the volunteers who served there. In spite of the fact that for a long time the Spanish Army had been class ridden, where officers rarely established personal ties with their men, the Blue Division proved to be an exception. Those who served as lieutenants, captains and majors maintained close contact with the men who served under them throughout their lives.

Although the defeat of Germany in 1945 obliged Franco's regime to minimise the importance of the Blue Division as far as possible, it proved impossible to do so. With the onset of the Cold war, being anti-communist no longer held any stigma; as a result, Blue Division Veteran's Associations sprang up all over Spain with thousands of members. The many public reunions were attended by men who had by then reached the rank of general (on the right of the illustration is a lieutenant-general) as well as former volunteers who had returned to civilian life or occupied modest positions in life. Those who continued to be members of the Falange wore their blue shirts and, if members of the so-called 'National Movement' (the name adopted by the Falange later on during Franco's regime), their more elaborate uniforms (such as the figure on the right). Many proudly displayed the decorations they had won in Russia. Although Wehrmacht insignia could no longer be worn with military uniform, the Falangists continued to display them on their blue shirts and the Blue Division shield was always worn. Like many other armies, the Spanish Army awarded long-service decorations to those who served any length of time in its elite units (such as the Legion). However, the only long-service badge worn on the arm was the shield of the Blue Division. Franco's government did little to celebrate the service of the Blue Division, mainly because from the end of World War II this would have been politically incorrect in the eyes of western public opinion. Nevertheless, the veterans of the Russian campaign always felt deep pride for having participated in the 'crusade against communism'.

The flag of the Barcelona Association of Blue Division Combatants, during one of the organisation's parades. (FDA)

Collections, museums and re-enactment groups

Given the official government policy, only a small room was given over to the Blue Division in the Spanish Army Museum, which was opened in the 1960s. The Asturian Blue Division Veterans' Association has its own museum. During the 1990s, the Blue Division Foundation opened an impressive museum, which unfortunately later closed. Its exhibits were handed over to the Spanish Army Museum, which is no longer located in Madrid, having been moved to the city of Toledo. However, the museum is still not open, and it will be necessary to wait for the museum inauguration to see what space is dedicated to the Blue Division. Therefore, at present, there is no public museum showing exhibits from the Blue Division; a few important, private collections do exist, though.

Re-enactment is a hobby that has only recently taken root in Spain. There are a few groups that have decided to represent the Blue Division. However, as in Spain this is a subject that tends to arouse political passions, these groups are small. The fear of the accusation of being apologists for Fascism keeps their activities limited.

CAIDOS EN LA DIVISION AZUL

CORRAL DE AYLLON †. CRESCENCIANO DIEGO G.
MIGUELANEZ †. TEODORO DOMINGO S.
SANTA-M^a DE NIEVA †. JUSTO DOMINGUEZ DE A.

VALSECA †. VICENTE DOMINGUEZ C.
FRESNEDA DE CUELLAR †. RUFINO DE LA FUENTE A.
TUREGANO †. LUCIANO GONZALEZ G.

VILLACASTIN †. ESTEBAN HEREDERO V.
LA CUESTA †. GERVASIO MARTIN G.
HONTALBILLA †. CELEDONIO MARTIN R.

VEGANZONES †. MARIANO MATESANZ B.
DONHIERRO † FRANCISCO

During Franco's regime, the names of Nationalist soldiers who fell in the Civil War were carved on the walls of churches. The Blue Division's fallen were also granted this right. The names seen here are of men from many of the small villages of the province of Segovia, in Castile. There were few Spanish towns and villages that did not lose at least one son in Russia. (FDA)

BIBLIOGRAPHY

The history of the Blue Division has been the object of study by many Spanish historians. These books tend to either praise or condemn the formation depending on the political ideology of the writer. However, universities in Spain have long been averse to the study of military history and the Blue Division has been explored more for its political and diplomatic significance than in purely military terms. Therefore, the most important work on the subject continues to be that by the American professors G. Kleinfeld and L.A. Tambs, *Hitler's Spanish Legion: the Blue Division in Russia*, published in 1979. British, French, German, Italian and even Polish authors have also published works on the Blue Division.

In Spanish, we have a large number of memoirs published by veterans (totalling nearly one hundred). Some of these veterans have gone further, writing authentic chronicles of the Blue Division, such as the books by Tomás Salvador (*Division 250*) or Fernando Vadillo's complete series of six titles covering the Blue Division's history from its origins to the return of prisoners (*Orillas del Voljov, Arrabales de Leningrado, Lucharon en Krasny Bor, Los legionarios, Los irreductibles* and *Los prisioneros*).

There is also a number of specialised texts written by Spanish military historians that include battalion histories, studies on recruitment for the division by regions in Spain, in-depth analysis of battles, etc. – and even a title dedicated to the study of the Blue Division from the perspective of stamp collecting! There is at present a renewed interest in the subject with the frequent publication of new books, such as an outstanding photographic history. There are also internet forums (*http://memoriablau.foros.ws* being the most interesting). Very few veterans are still alive, but there are hundreds of thousands of Spaniards who had a family member in the Blue Division and this episode in their country's history generates passionate interest.

INDEX

References to illustrations are shown in **bold**. Plates are prefixed pl, with captions on the page in brackets.

Panzer Tactical Signs 1935-42

Panzer Div HQ

Division CP

Pz Brigade HQ

1st Pz Regt.

2nd Pz Regt.

4th Pz Battn. (I/I-II/2)

Staff Co.

Medium Tank Co.

Armoured Workshop Co.

Panzer Tactical Signs 1943-45

Panzer Div HQ

Pz Regt HQ

Staff Co

and

Panzer Abteilungen
(Panzer Battalions)

Armoured Supply Co.

PzKpfw IV Tank Co.

Armoured Workshop Co.

Panzer Division signs 1939-1945

Poland, 1939

Poland
(low visibilty variant)

1940-1942, Standard

1940-1945, Variant

1943-1945, Variant

North Africa, Variant

1940-1945, Variant

**National
Insignia**

**Command
Pennants**

Panzer Group
(Panzergruppe)

Panzer Division

Panzer Brigade

Panzer Regiment

Panzer Battalion
(Panzer Abteilung)

**Turret
Numbers**

Afrika Korps insignia variants

© Nigel Pell.

1941-42   1942   Kursk   1943-45

——— Leibstandarte SS Adolf Hitler ———

1942-45   Kursk   1944   1944

——— Das Reich ———   ——— Hohenstaufen ———

1942-45   Kursk   Kursk

——— Totenkopf ———

1941-42   1941-42   1942   1943-44   1944-45

——— Wiking ———

1942-45   Kursk   Kursk

———Frundsberg———

1943   1944   1944   1944

——— Reichsführer SS ———   —— Hitlerjugend ——   —— Götz von Berlichingen ——

Key to Division signs page 93

(note all were painted in yellow unless stated.)

1. 1st Panzer Division - 1940-45. Note 1940-45 insignia introduced for operation Citadel, later used with an invertedY (white).

2. 2nd Panzer Division - 1943-45 in white.

3. 3rd Panzer Division: black on white or sometimes in red. White shield with black bear.

4. 4th Panzer Division

5. 5th Panzer Division - often painted on a black square.

6. 6th Panzer Division

7. 7th Panzer Division

8. 8th Panzer Division

9. 9th Panzer Division

10. 10th Panzer Division

11. 11th Panzer Division - 1941-45 in white.

12. 12th Panzer Division

13. 13th Panzer Division

14. 14th Panzer Division

15. 15th Panzer Division - painted in red, white or black. After 1943 in white.

16. 16th Panzer Division - also on yellow-edged, black shield.

17. 17th Panzer Division

18. 18th Panzer Division

19. 19th Panzer Division

20. 20th Panzer Division

21. 21st Panzer Division - painted in white.

22. 22nd Panzer Division

23. 23rd Panzer Division - also painted in white and used with tower-shaped sign.

24. 24th Panzer Division

25. 25th Panzer Division- shield painted in red with yellow stars and a black bar.

26. 26th Panzer Division: painted in white.

27. 27th Panzer Division

28. 116th Panzer Division -1944 painted in white 1943-45 painted in solid or outline white.